Esther Trépanier

Translated by Judith Terry

Scott Brandtner Eveleigh Webber: Revisiting Montreal Abstraction of the 1940s

McGill-Queen's University Press
Montreal & Kingston • London • Chicago

Les Presses de l'Université de Montréal
Montreal

Musée d'art de Joliette
Joliette

Published simultaneously in French as
Scott, Brandtner, Eveleigh, Webber: revoir l'abstraction montréalaise des années 1940
by the Presses de l'Université de Montréal

ISBN 978-0-2280-1595-6 (paper)
ISBN 978-0-2280-1596-3 (ePDF)

Legal deposit fourth quarter 2022
Bibliothèque nationale du Québec

Printed in Canada

Canada — Canada Council for the Arts / Conseil des arts du Canada

We acknowledge the support of the Canada Council for the Arts.
Nous remercions le Conseil des arts du Canada de son soutien.

Library and Archives Canada Cataloguing in Publication

Title: Scott, Brandtner, Eveleigh, Webber : revisiting Montreal abstraction of the 1940s / Esther Trépanier ; translated by Judith Terry.

Other titles: Oubliés. English

Names: Trépanier, Esther, 1951- author.

Description: Translation of: Oubliés: Brandtner, Eveleigh, Scott, Webber : revoir l'abstraction montréalaise des années 1940. | Includes bibliographical references and index.

Identifiers: Canadiana (print) 20220244995 | Canadiana (ebook) 20220245053 | ISBN 9780228015956 (softcover) | ISBN 9780228015963 (ePDF)

Subjects: LCSH: Brandtner, Fritz, 1896-1969—Criticism and interpretation. | LCSH: Eveleigh, Henry, 1909-1999—Criticism and interpretation. | LCSH: Scott, Marian Dale, 1906-1993—Criticism and interpretation. | LCSH: Webber, Gordon McKinley, 1909-1965—Criticism and interpretation. | LCSH: Painting, Abstract—Québec (Province)—Montréal—History and criticism. | LCSH: Painting, Abstract—Québec (Province)—Montréal—History—20th century. | LCSH: Painters—Québec (Province)—Montréal—History—20th century.

Classification: LCC ND245.5.A28 T7413 2022 | DDC 759.114/28—dc23

Contents

Foreword

In writing classes in elementary school, the very first thing we learn is that every story should have a beginning, a middle, and an end. The linearity of storytelling is presented as primordial to people's understanding. And most often the second rule we are taught is to not introduce too many characters at once – again, so that readers may easily understand and relate to the context and the key players. In a lot of ways, our official written history is much the same in its construction. That is why we have art history books that are relatively simplified and linear. Artist A influences artist B, who influences artist C, and so forth. But is that really how history unfolds? Is that how we live?

As I write these lines, I have just spent a week at the Venice Biennale. With thousands of contemporary artists from around the world exhibiting simultaneously on an island of barely five square kilometres, the Venice Biennale makes the complexity and diversity of the world extremely apparent. Try as you might to find one, no true common thread or linearity exists in this diversity. Critics can, and will most surely attempt to, draw a metanarrative from all that diversity. But to do so will be to forget the majority of the art that was presented. Discussing all of the art presented in Venice would require too much time and would not be very comprehensible; choices therefore need to be made. But these choices will have important repercussions for how any specific period is recorded and remembered by future generations.

For years, Esther Trépanier has dedicated much of her research to better understanding how the Montreal art scene of the first half of the twentieth century came to be. It was a rich and multi-faceted period that, in most history books, has been oversimplified at the cost of some of its important components.

Preface and Acknowledgments

This book accompanies the exhibition *Forgotten! Scott, Brandtner, Eveleigh, Webber: Revisiting Montreal Abstraction of the 1940s*, organized by the Musée d'art de Joliette. The idea of taking a fresh look at abstraction in Montreal during the 1940s grew out of a talk I gave as part of the annual lectures I have had the pleasure of presenting at the Montreal Museum of Fine Arts over the past several years. In 2018, the third lecture of a series titled "Quand l'œuvre sort de sa réserve" examined the relation between modern Montreal artists and war via a study of *War Commentary*, a work by Henry Eveleigh that the museum had acquired in 2015. As I prepared my talk, I was once again forced to recognize that a number of artists have been "forgotten" by Quebec art history, including several anglophones who were exhibiting abstract works during the 1940s at the same time as the Automatistes.

Realizing that this was a subject sufficiently far-reaching and compelling to warrant an exhibition and a publication, I submitted an exhibition proposal to the Musée d'art de Joliette, whose courage and enthusiasm I must immediately applaud. Courage is certainly required to produce a historical exhibition, with all this implies logistically – including the management of loans, the design of a suitable expositional space, and the planning of a tour – without access to the financial and human resources of a major museum. As for enthusiasm, the indefatigable dynamism with which the project has been received and guided to completion through every stage by the Musée's director, Jean-François Bélisle, and curator Julie Alary Lavallée (and before her Émilie Grandmont-Bérubé and Marie-Claude Landry), along with Nathalie Galego, has been extremely precious to me. I would also like to express my gratitude to all the Musée's various teams, including those in communications, education, visitor services, and technical installation, who have worked toward the success of the exhibition. My heartfelt thanks, as well, to the lenders and staff of various museums who have facilitated the loan of works and their inclusion in the exhibition tour.

This project, which focuses on a lesser-known facet of our history, is grounded in considerable research, whose results it would have been a shame to leave unpublished. I am therefore most grateful for the contributions of those who have made this book possible, notably the teams at the Presses de l'Université de Montréal (PUM) and McGill-Queen's University Press, who agreed to a co-publication in collaboration with the Musée d'art de Joliette. They include Patrick Poirier, director of the PUM, Jonathan Crago, editor-in-chief of McGill-Queen's University Press, and Sylvie Brousseau, project manager at the PUM. I wish to extend particularly warm thanks to Guy Champagne, senior editor at the PUM, who has supervised the publication process.

Many people have been of invaluable help at various points during my research. I am especially grateful to Lucie Charbonneau, collector and guide at the Montreal Museum of Fine Arts, who not only shared with me important research on Gordon Webber on which she has been working for a number of years, but also proved of great assistance in establishing the list of exhibitions in which the artists under study participated. Several graduate students at the Université du Québec à Montréal have also contributed, including Marie-Lise Poirier, who brought her methodological rigour to bear on the revision of the bibliographical references and a reading of the first draft of the manuscript, and Myriem Alami, Marie-Maxime de Andrade, and Véronique Lemaître-Beaulieu, who also helped on various aspects of the research. My thanks to them. I would be remiss if I failed to include among their number Marie Faugnon, museologist and scenographic designer, for her crucial assistance in conceiving the exhibition's layout.

Any manuscript destined for publication can benefit from the enlightened comments of early readers. Those offered by Louise Joubert, Julie Alary Lavallée, and two (anonymous) evaluators engaged by the PUM enabled me to improve the text of this study. I am very grateful to them, and to Judith Terry, for her attentive reading and brilliant translation.

The search for works and information and the acquisition of photographs to illustrate a book and document an exhibition is a long and arduous process, particularly during a pandemic. I would like to acknowledge the vital support of the curatorial, photographic, and rights and licences departments of the

Art Gallery of Hamilton, the Art Gallery of Ontario, the Art Gallery of Windsor, the Musée d'art contemporain de Montréal, the National Gallery of Canada, the Montreal Museum of Fine Arts, the Canadian War Museum, the Musée national des beaux-arts du Québec, the McGill University Visual Arts Collection, McGill University Library, and the Archives nationales du Québec.

For their particular help, warmest thanks to Suzan Eveleigh, Pagan Eveleigh, and Véronique Morisset; Marc Bellemare, Sandria P. Bouliane, Danielle Doucet, the late and much lamented François-Marc Gagnon, Sébastien Hudon, Alain Laforest, Vincent Pelsser, and Richard Webber; to Jacques Des Rochers, Richard Gagnier, and Marie-Claude Saia (all three of the Montreal Museum of Fine Arts); Nathalie Thibault (Musée national des beaux-arts du Québec); Gwendolyn Owens (McGill University Visual Arts Collection); Jennifer Garland (McGill University Library, John Bland Canadian Architecture Collection, Gordon Webber fonds); Marie-Eve Beaupré (Musée d'art contemporain); Paul Maréchal (Power Corporation Collection); Lise Bizzoni (Centre de recherche interuniversitaire sur la littérature et la culture québécoises – CRILCQ); and to the gallerists Éric Devlin and Isadore Rubinfeld (Kastel Gallery). A very special thank you also to Brian Merrett for his invaluable contribution to the research and production of photographic documents.

Finally, I extend my gratitude to the organizations whose financial support has made the publication of this book and the presentation of the exhibition possible: the Museums Assistance Program of the Department of Canadian Heritage; the Programme de soutien à l'édition du CRILCQ; and the Programme "Mobilisation et diffusion des connaissances et soutien à la publication" of the arts faculty of UQAM.

I salute all those mentioned here, as well as any I may have inadvertently omitted. To be able to present the results of one's research to a broad public in the form of an exhibition and a catalogue is, for an art historian, a source of real joy.

Esther Trépanier

Introduction

Each society has its own history and its own rate of development, whether on the economic, social, intellectual, or cultural fronts. Consequently, each history must be assessed in terms of its own specificity. For example, unlike France, Italy, Germany, and a number of other countries, neither Quebec nor Canada saw the emergence during the early twentieth century of such avant-garde art movements as Cubism, Futurism, and Expressionism. An openness – still tentative – to some aspects of these European modernist trends would not be discernible in Quebec until the late 1930s.

As a result, the history of art followed a different path in Quebec, where serious consideration of the notion of modern art did not get under way until the interwar period. This reflection was conducted, sometimes rather awkwardly, by critics writing about art practices that, although still figurative, were gradually moving away from the Impressionism and landscape painting that had been the first signs of a cautious break with academic art. The influence of post-Impressionism and even Fauvism, the choice of more varied subjects, and a less nationalist approach to landscape would characterize the works of artists affiliated with the informal Beaver Hall Group, founded in 1920, and even more markedly those of the next generation, several members of which would, in 1939, become founding members of the Contemporary Arts Society.[1] Their innovative practices would be reviewed by art critics who, in their coverage of the Montreal art scene, saw modernity in terms of artists' freedom to represent subjects of their choice, using techniques that conveyed their subjective vision. Modern artists were those who had thrown off the yoke not only of academic rules but also of any ideology that glorified the land and the nation. Reviews sympathetic to a more contemporary perspective had appeared in a few newspapers during the 1920s, but it was not until the following decade that a group of critics, composed of both francophones and anglophones, would open the debate on what was called "living art." This concept signified art that was "of its time," reflecting the era while exploring new formal issues.[2] By the end

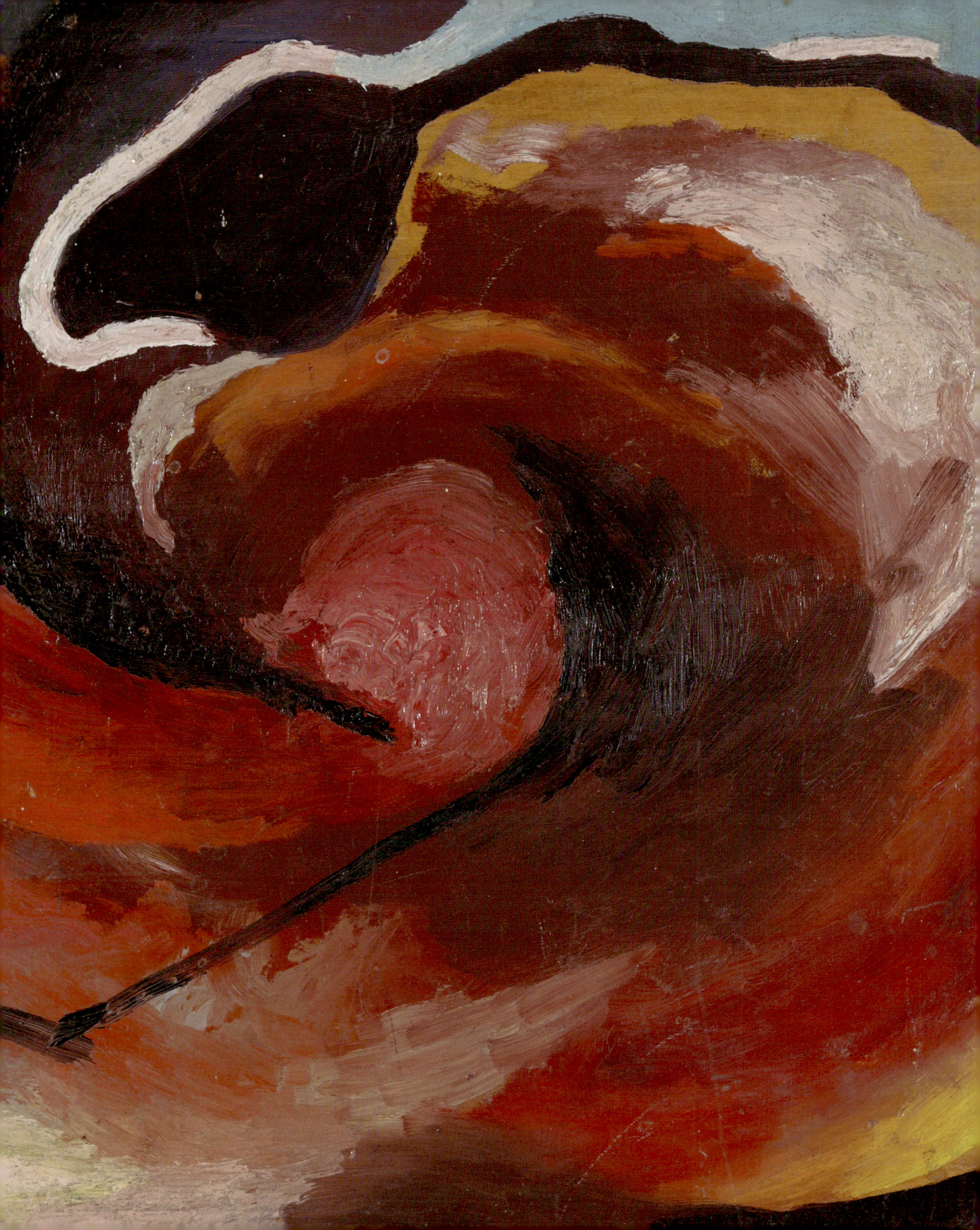

of the 1930s, partially under the impetus of works being exhibited by artists like Fritz Brandtner and Marian Dale Scott, ideas about Cubism, Expressionism, and occasionally abstraction were beginning to become part of the discussion.

The real turning point, however, came in the 1940s. When the Contemporary Arts Society was created in 1939, most of the artists among its founding members were linked to the anglophone community, and most were still attached to figurative art, even if they had adopted a more modern, non-academic approach. But three of them, Marian Dale Scott (1906–1993),[3] Fritz Brandtner (1896–1969), and Henry Rowland Eveleigh (1909–1999), stood out from the rest, for critics often employed the term "abstraction" to characterize the formal audacity of their pictures, even if they were not always, strictly speaking, non-objective. In 1943, Gordon McKinley Webber (1909–1965) settled in Montreal and began exhibiting works that were even more resolutely abstract. These four anglophone artists, whose practices stimulated reflection among Montreal critics on the meaning of abstraction, would nevertheless soon be overshadowed by the emergence from the francophone community of new players, who would decisively command the attention of critics interested in contemporary art.

On his return from Europe in 1940, Alfred Pellan (1906–1988) brought with him a large number of abstract, Cubist, and Surrealist works, and he rapidly became a key reference among young francophone artists and critics alike. Before long, however, his position as the "herald" of modern art would be contested by Paul-Émile Borduas (1905–1960) and his group, who advocated a different approach. Although rooted originally in French Surrealism, their vision gradually moved away from this source, and they began defending a form of automatist painting based not on any preconceived idea but on the spontaneous impulse of an initial gesture, around which the artist would structure the work. A marked stylistic unity among members of the Automatiste group and the radical tone of their manifesto, *Refus global*, published in 1948, gave them genuine avant-garde status. In order to impose their vision of art as the only truly original path, the Automatistes felt compelled to break completely with the past – even the very recent past, which included Pellan and most of the members of the Contemporary Arts Society. The rupture urged by the Automatistes came just

Henry Eveleigh
Untitled (detail), about 1942
ill. 49, page 106

as Pellan and his followers were defending an opposing position in their own manifesto, *Prisme d'yeux*. Produced a few months before *Refus global*, it expressed a desire to "bring together the healthy forces" of painting, and to unite all the groups seeking "the affirmation of independent art" via the multiple avenues of "the pictorial experience of each individual."[4]

The short first chapter of this book describes the context in which the question of abstraction first emerged in Quebec during the late 1930s, noting especially the unity/exclusion dichotomy that split the contemporary art milieu of the 1940s. It recalls how abstraction was also being explored by anglophone artists exhibiting in Montreal throughout that decade, even though art history has focused most of its attention on francophone contributions, particularly those of the Automatistes, who are often seen as the "founders" of abstraction in Quebec. In fact, despite the significance of the artistic emancipation that both Borduas and Pellan triggered among young creators, the history of art of the 1940s cannot be limited to these two artists and their respective groups, and consequently remains, as yet, largely unwritten. The work of a host of Montreal artists from diverse linguistic and cultural communities has still to be thoroughly researched. This study does not seek to look in depth at all the issues raised by this decade, which include the debates surrounding art and war, the continuation of a number of modern figurative practices, and the complex web of networks[5] that linked both famous and lesser-known artists. More modestly, this book aims to examine the question of abstract art in Montreal[6] aside from the numerous, well-documented controversies that accompanied the advent of the Automatiste group.[7] While not denying its importance, it seems to me that the development of abstract art in Quebec cannot be reduced to this movement alone. My aim here is to highlight the contribution to abstraction of four anglophone artists – one woman, Marian Dale Scott, and three men, Fritz Brandtner, Henry Eveleigh, and Gordon Webber. It is a humble objective, but a crucial one, for their practices had an impact on the history of Quebec abstraction, although that impact has so far gone unrecognized.[8]

The second chapter concentrates on the four artists' individual practices and explores how their works nourished the idea of abstraction as understood in the 1940s. This understanding was remarkably fluid, since the concept was not applied exclusively to non-figurative art. What these anglophone painters brought to the Quebec art scene were allusions to international trends that went beyond the influence of Paris. Marian Dale Scott's aesthetic influences often came from American or British art. Since the 1930s, Fritz Brandtner had been introducing the art-going public to Expressionism, and even pure abstraction. Toward the end of that decade, Henry Eveleigh exhibited works inspired by both Cubism and Surrealism, and then, in the early 1940s, executed a number of paintings in a gestural abstract style. Finally, the Bauhaus-influenced works exhibited by Gordon Webber embodied a form of geometric abstraction that combined the dynamics of line, colour, and design with an experimental approach to materials. The second chapter looks closely at these works, but it also explores their critical reception, since it is in the writings of the art critics of the time that the multiple meanings of the word "abstraction" are most clearly revealed. To close this section, I discuss a few works from the 1950s, simply to give readers a glimpse of the continuities and breaks that shaped these artists' subsequent careers.[9]

The third chapter examines the social and political context in which the four artists were working. It highlights their eagerness to quit the "ivory tower," a metaphor used often to describe the studio where artists traditionally cloister themselves in search of the tranquility required to meditate on and resolve creative questions. Their impulse was, on the contrary, to extricate art from its usual rarefied surroundings and to democratize it, to make it accessible to as wide an audience as possible. Having experienced the Depression, and living now in a time of war, these artists were determined to be involved in their own way in the major struggles and issues of the era. Scott, Brandtner, Eveleigh, and Webber did not all meet this challenge in the same fashion, but meet it they did – by producing works that portrayed the war, by executing public murals, by promoting art education among the disadvantaged, and by developing projects that reflected postwar ideals. Without seeking to be exhaustive, this chapter reviews a few of these achievements, which constitute not only a distinguishing feature of the anglophone art community of the time but also an example of the remarkable aesthetic diversity that characterized Montreal's art scene during the 1940s.[10]

Without doing full justice to the decade in all its complexity, this study of four anglophone painters associated with abstraction and of the time in which they were working has at least the virtue of drawing attention to the richness of a period in the history of art that remains largely unexplored.

Fritz Brandtner
Design No. 6 (detail), n.d.
ill. 32, page 83

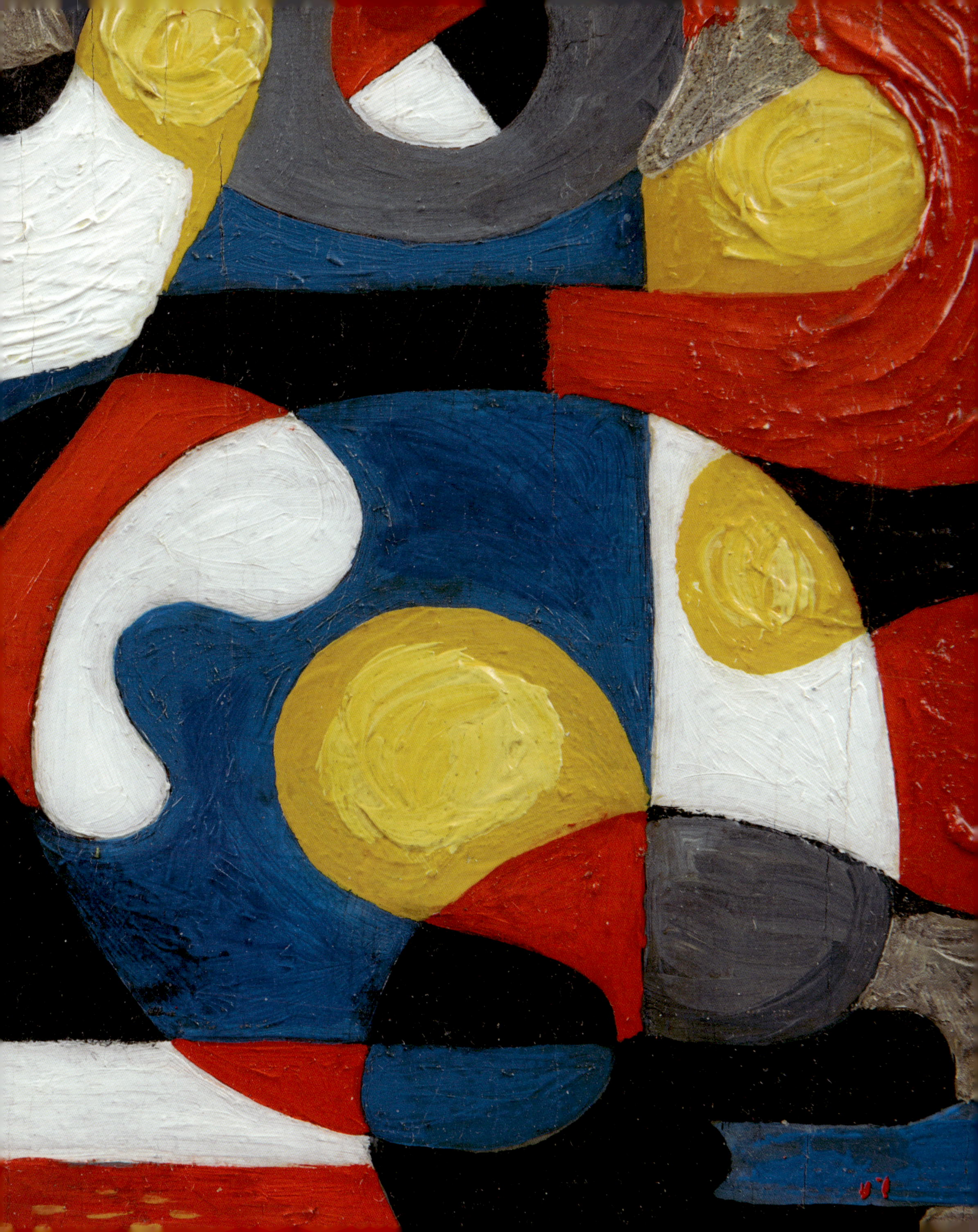

Notes

1 On the Beaver Hall Group, see Jacques Des Rochers and Brian Foss, eds., *1920s Modernism in Montreal: The Beaver Hall Group*, exhib. cat. (Montreal: The Montreal Museum of Fine Arts/London: Black Dog Publishing, 2015); on the Contemporary Arts Society, see Christopher Varley, *The Contemporary Arts Society, Montreal, 1939–1948/La Contemporary Arts Society, Montréal, 1939–1948*, exhib. cat. (Edmonton: Edmonton Art Gallery, 1980).

2 For more on these modern critics, see Esther Trépanier, *Peinture et modernité au Québec, 1919–1939* (Quebec City: Éditions Nota bene, 1998).

3 Throughout the text, the birth and death dates of Canadian artists only are given.

4 The *Prisme d'yeux* manifesto possesses neither the coherence nor the scope of *Refus global*, which includes several essays. Nor was it formally published: it took the form of a pamphlet of fewer than 450 words produced to accompany an exhibition presented by the group on 4 February 1948 in an annex of the Art Association of Montreal. A transcription of the original is available online at: http://www.conseildesarts.org/documents/Manisfeste/manifeste_prisme_dyeux.htm (accessed 10 January 2021).

5 The four artists who are the focus of this study belonged to a number of the same artistic, social, and political networks. Scott was a close friend of Brandtner, but also of Norman Bethune and John Lyman, and they all attended the weekly salons held by the latter. Eveleigh was, like the other three, a member of the Contemporary Arts Society, but he also had links to the graphic design milieu. Webber moved in architectural circles, but also knew people in the world of set decoration. And among other things, all participated regularly in the same group exhibitions, and all taught. More extended research into these numerous networks would undoubtedly have the effect of revealing the cultural richness of Montreal's anglophone community.

6 In Toronto, several painters also exhibited abstract works well before the creation of the Painters Eleven collective. They include Bertram Brooker (1888–1955), who showed abstractions in the late 1920s, and Lawren Harris (1885–1970) and Edna Taçon (1905–1980), both of whom were making non-figurative art in the 1930s. See, for example, Roald Nasgaard, *Abstract Painting in Canada* (Vancouver: Douglas & McIntyre/Halifax: Art Gallery of Nova Scotia, 2007).

7 I would like to pay tribute here to the exceptionally well-documented publications of my late colleague, the art historian François-Marc Gagnon. Among his many works, of particular interest here are *Chronique du mouvement automatiste québécois, 1941–1954* (Montreal: Lanctôt Éditeur, 1998) and his essay "Le sens du mot 'abstraction' dans la critique d'art et les déclarations des peintres des années quarante au Québec," in Yvan Lamonde and Esther Trépanier, eds., *L'avènement de la modernité culturelle au Québec* (Quebec City: Institut québécois de recherche sur la culture, 1986 [2007]).

8 Aside from a handful of exhibition catalogues, which will be referred to in the chapters to come, and a few, often brief, mentions in general studies of the history of abstraction in Canada, there has so far been no study that takes a serious look at their contribution to the development of abstract art in Quebec during the 1940s.

9 I cannot explore the 1950s in any depth, since it would require taking account of other groups, such as the post-Automatistes and the Plasticiens, as well as the new sites of diffusion that emerged in the postwar period and the transformations they engendered in the critical discourse. This is a whole other area of research, and there already exist a number of studies on different aspects and artists of this period.

10 Other artists across Canada were also interested in these questions. My study focuses on the Montreal art scene, which was one of the most active in the country, in order to show that its actors were not exclusively francophone. This conclusion also lay at the heart of my monograph on the city's Jewish artists, *Jewish Painters of Montreal: Witnesses of Their Time* (Montreal: Les Éditions de l'Homme, 2008).

There is a tradition in art history that tends to equate abstraction with non-objective art. Although the avant-garde art movements that emerged after the Second World War and a theoretical perspective grounded in formalism reinforced this alignment, the concept of abstraction, before becoming crystallized in non-representation, was nevertheless applied to a range of art practices and approaches. This was especially true in 1940s Quebec, where the word "abstraction" did not become part of art critical discourse until the late 1930s.

CHAPTER 1

The Origins of Abstraction in Quebec: A Contextualization

Anyone exploring the different meanings assigned to the term "abstract" should proceed with caution. It is vital to situate oneself in the period under study: with a few rare exceptions, its art critics had only the most cursory knowledge of international avant-garde movements. Although a handful knew something of Cubism – and maybe even Surrealism – as practised in France, the majority were quite ignorant of the complex issues surrounding abstraction. This partially explains their problems in writing about it. But in fact art critics publishing at the time in Montreal's major newspapers rarely got involved in serious aesthetic discussions. All too often, they simply listed the artists and works that had captured their attention at a given exhibition, without really explaining why. Occasionally, though, there were those who went a little deeper, and their accounts shed some light on the various viewpoints prevailing at the time.

The Appearance in the 1930s of the Word "Abstraction"

From the mid-1930s on, the concept of abstraction began featuring in discussions about Fritz Brandtner, a German-born artist who would make Montreal his home from 1934 until his death in 1969. Brandtner saw art as an adventure that offered enormous possibilities for experimentation. "All creative great art is of an experimental nature," he wrote in his journal. "The only art work of no value is that which is not experimental."[1] It was a vision clearly reflected in his practice, which simultaneously exploited the vocabularies of Expressionism, Cubism, and non-figurative art, as witness such paintings as *Bathing*, 1937, *The Montreal Harbour*, 1938, and *Abstraction,* 1930.

In February 1936, Brandtner, who was a friend of the Communist doctor Norman Bethune,[2] held a solo exhibition, in the gallery of the Henry Morgan department store in Montreal, which had been sponsored by the Canadian League against War and Fascism. A number of the 120 works on view were in an Expressionist style, and a few veered close to abstraction.

The exhibition sparked a certain controversy. Robert Ayre of the *Gazette* praised the artist's vitality and intensity, declaring that Brandtner used the visible world simply as a springboard to launch himself into an adventure of shapes, rhythms, colours, and emotions.[3] Ayre characterized Brandtner as an Expressionist, situating his approach within the parameters of a broad view of abstraction that defined it as reinterpretation – the formal reorganization of elements drawn from the visible world. The less informed Reynald (pseudonym of Éphrem-Réginald Bertrand), art critic for *La Presse*, was nothing like so enthusiastic. While his article, titled "Les cauchemars de Fritz Brandtner," acknowledged that the artist's "nightmares and hallucinations" were inspired by "the horror of war" – which certainly "fires the blood," but like a "bitter poison" – and described the painter as "vigorous, powerful and original," he nonetheless declared the work "brutal."[4] According to Reynald, Brandtner dismissed convention and ignored the rules of drawing and colour in order to "shock the bourgeoisie." A few days later, a colleague working for *Le Canada*, Henri Girard, responded to Reynald's review.[5] Girard came to the defence not only of the artist – whom he described as a "sincere interpreter of the

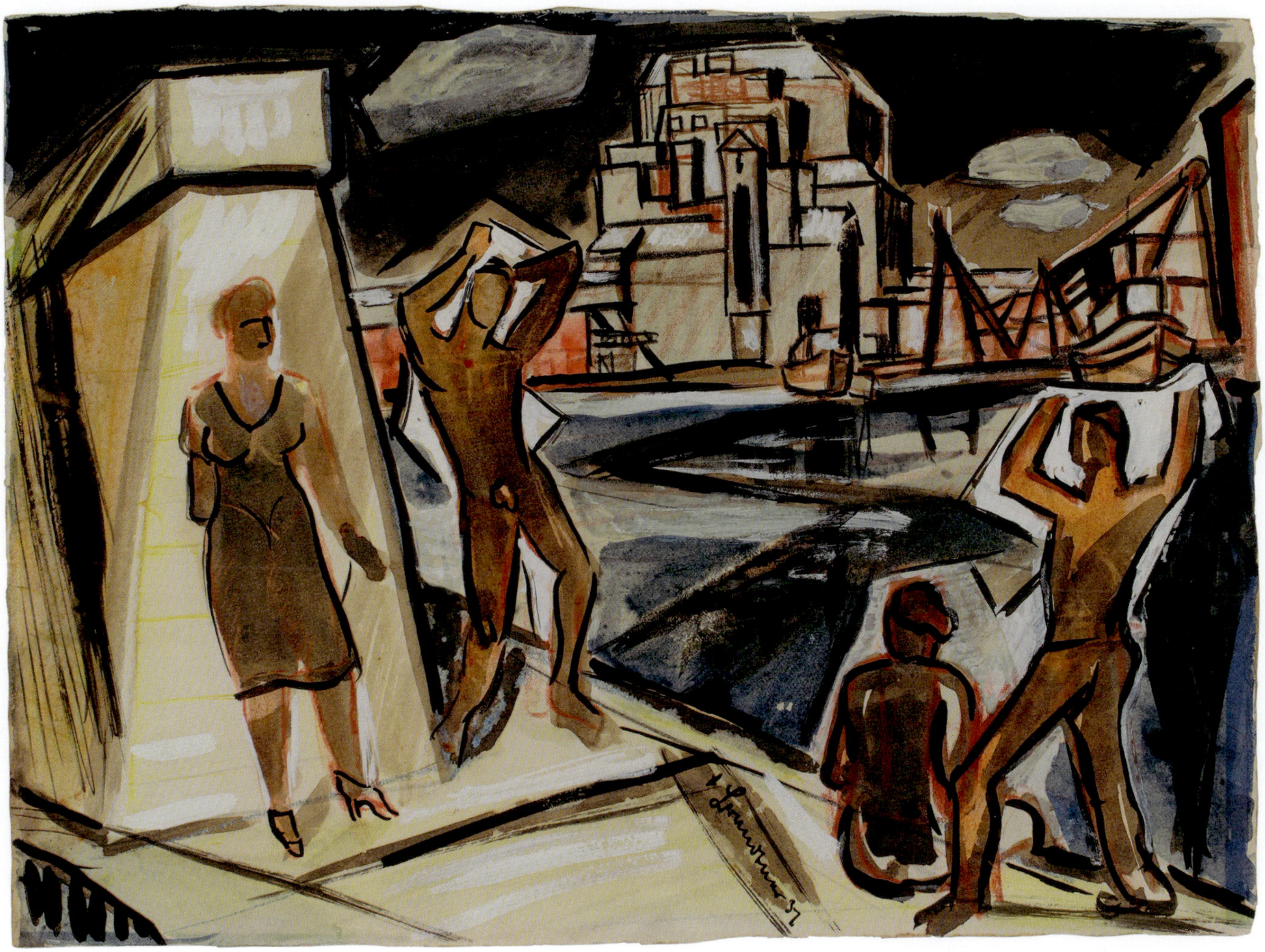

ill. 1
Fritz Brandtner
Bathing, 1937

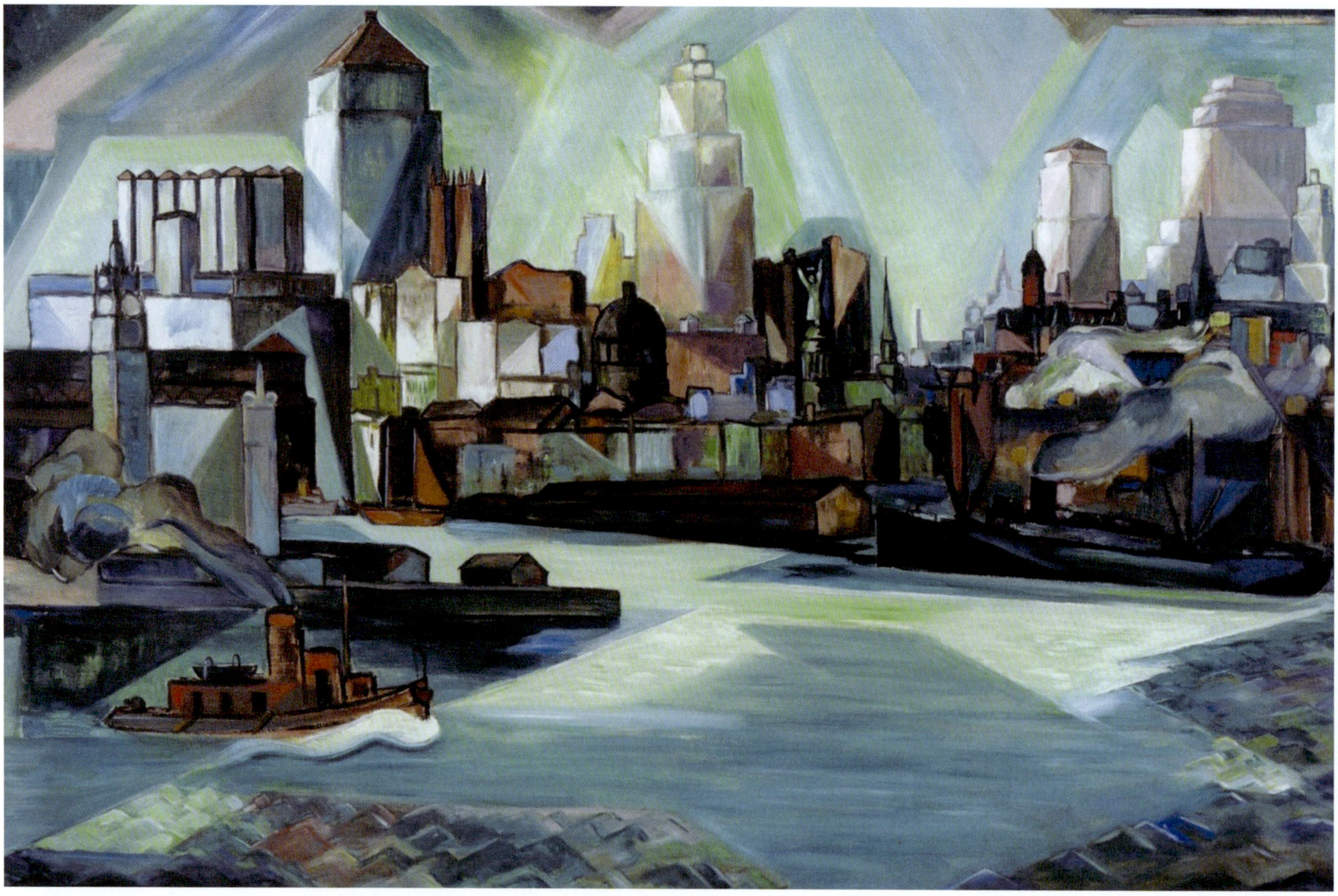

ill. 2
Fritz Brandtner
The Montreal Harbour, 1938

anxiety of our time" and a "true creator" – but also of living art. "For art," he wrote, "as long as it is living, is informed by neither stability nor well-defined principles. It lives and evolves. When it stays still, when it follows formulas, that's decadence." In Girard's opinion, Brandtner, had "the courage to paint in accordance with his own temperament, not, as has been thoughtlessly suggested, in order to offend the bourgeoisie, but rather without caring if they are offended or pleased."

In his advocacy on behalf of Montreal's modern artists, of all origins, Girard never missed an opportunity to attack the conservatism and chauvinism that still dominated the milieu. In an article titled "L'École de Paris," published that same year, 1936, in *Le Canada*,[6] he denounced the "xenophobia" and "narrow-mindedness" of his contemporaries, calling them "conservative," "ignorant," and "uncultivated," and ridiculing them for displaying their lack of knowledge "when abstract painting has been recognized in Europe for over thirty years and has shocked no one in the major cities of the United States for at least fifteen." So, at last, the hitherto ignored word was out: abstraction!

It is important to note that the classical humanist education received by the francophone critics, including Henri Girard, encouraged them for the most part to consider abstraction, like Surrealism, as a reflection of, at best, the "obscuring of the notion of man,"[7] and, at worst, the "decadence" of civilization. This was true for Girard, Reynald, and many others, among them the painter Jean Paul Lemieux (1904–1990), who in the late 1930s published a handful of articles in the newspaper *Le Jour*. A champion of modern Canadian art, Lemieux maintained that "the true work of art symbolizes the era in which the artist has lived … it is the image of a civilization and a synthesis of the ideas that distinguish it from others."[8] Nevertheless, although Lemieux paid tribute to Picasso, a "giant of contemporary art," and recognized that his works, like Pellan's, were representative of their time,[9] he rejected Surrealism and abstraction, writing:

> It [Surrealism] is a morbid, unwholesome art, entirely characteristic of our troubled era, an intense search for images from the subconscious. As for abstract art, it is a degeneration of Cubism, a combining of colour for colour's sake and form for form's sake, with no concern for the subject represented. Refinement of a decadent society.[10]

Lemieux was not alone: his skepticism was shared by a number of his contemporaries, all ambivalent about recent art trends (Surrealism and abstraction) that they associated with the "decadence" of civilization. The following remarks by Reynald effectively summarize his position:

> Individualists and sometimes gripers, but still more sincere than most, our own moderns – like all moderns – convey the sense of life as it is today. Is it their fault if that life is decadent and deranged? Isn't a sometimes sick but active imagination better than no imagination at all?[11]

There were a few critics, however, who took a more intellectually rigorous attitude toward contemporary art. One was Maurice Gagnon, who also taught art history and served as the curator of the École du meuble library, as well as organizing exhibitions of modern art. Basing his approach on the principle that the modernity of a work of art depended on the autonomy of its pictorialism in relation to reality, Gagnon wrote a series of articles in 1937 under the general title "Introduction to Modern Painting." The four essays, which focused on "Impressionism," "Cézanne, Gauguin and Van Gogh," "Fauvism," and "Expressionism and Cubism," can be seen as forerunners of the books he would publish in the 1940s.[12] Gagnon's series presented the history of modern art as evolutionary and progressing essentially according to a logic of "reaction." The synthesis of Cézanne, Gauguin, and Van Gogh was seen as challenging the superficial analysis of the Impressionists; the powerful consonances of the Fauves were a response to the "delicate harmonies" of a lingering Impressionism; with its abstract geometric constructions, Cubism was countering the Impressionist perception of "truth"; and Expressionism was exteriorizing human affect and resisting the "excess of abstract thinking" inherent in the abstract geometricism of the Cubist vision.

There are two points to be made here. The first is that, in 1937, there began emerging in Gagnon's writing (as it would later in Lemieux's) the idea that Cubism leads to abstraction. The second is that, for the critics of the time, Paris and its art movements were the only model, which led them to disregard the often more spiritualist abstract practices of painters like Kandinsky and Mondrian.

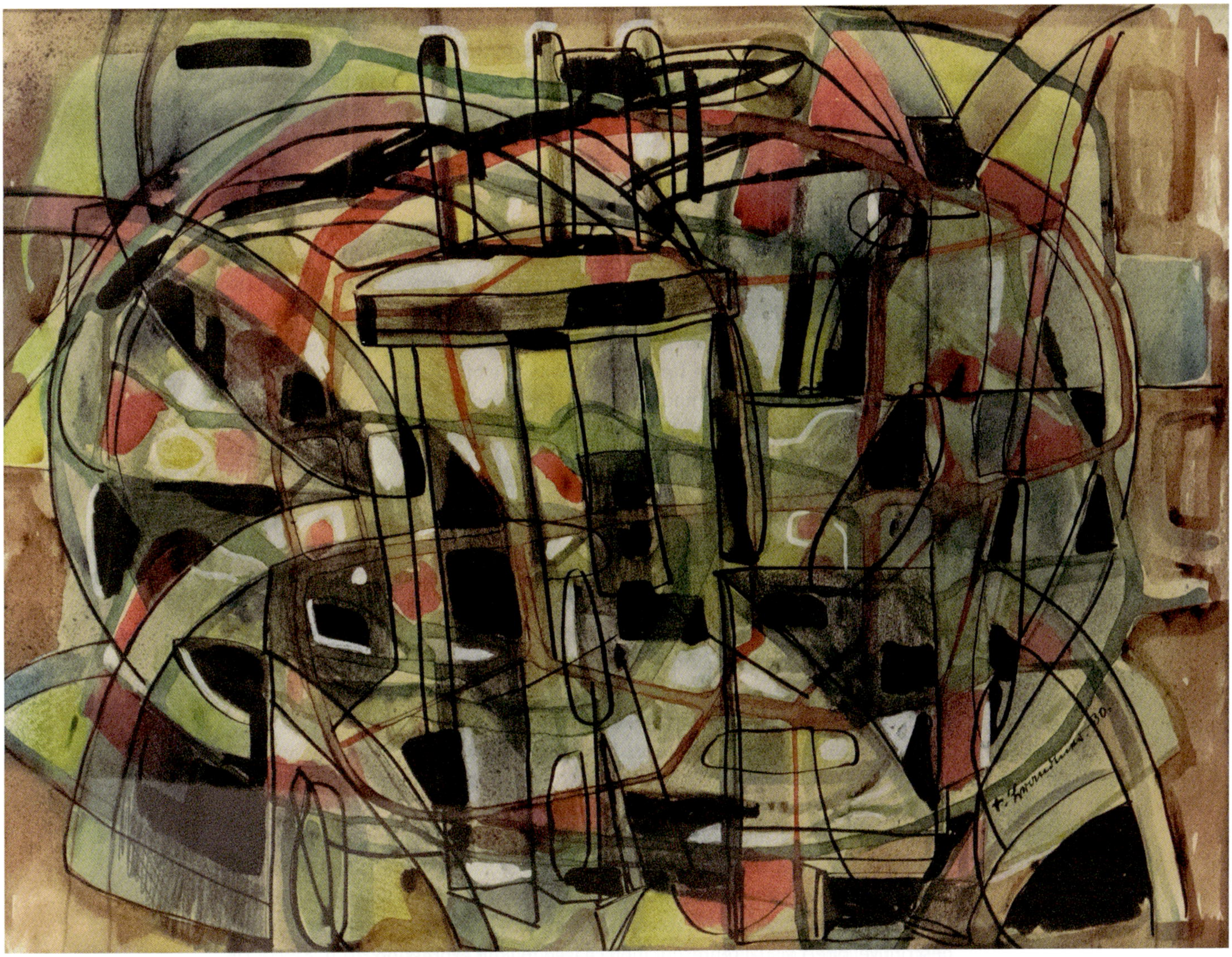

ill. 3
Fritz Brandtner
Abstraction, 1930

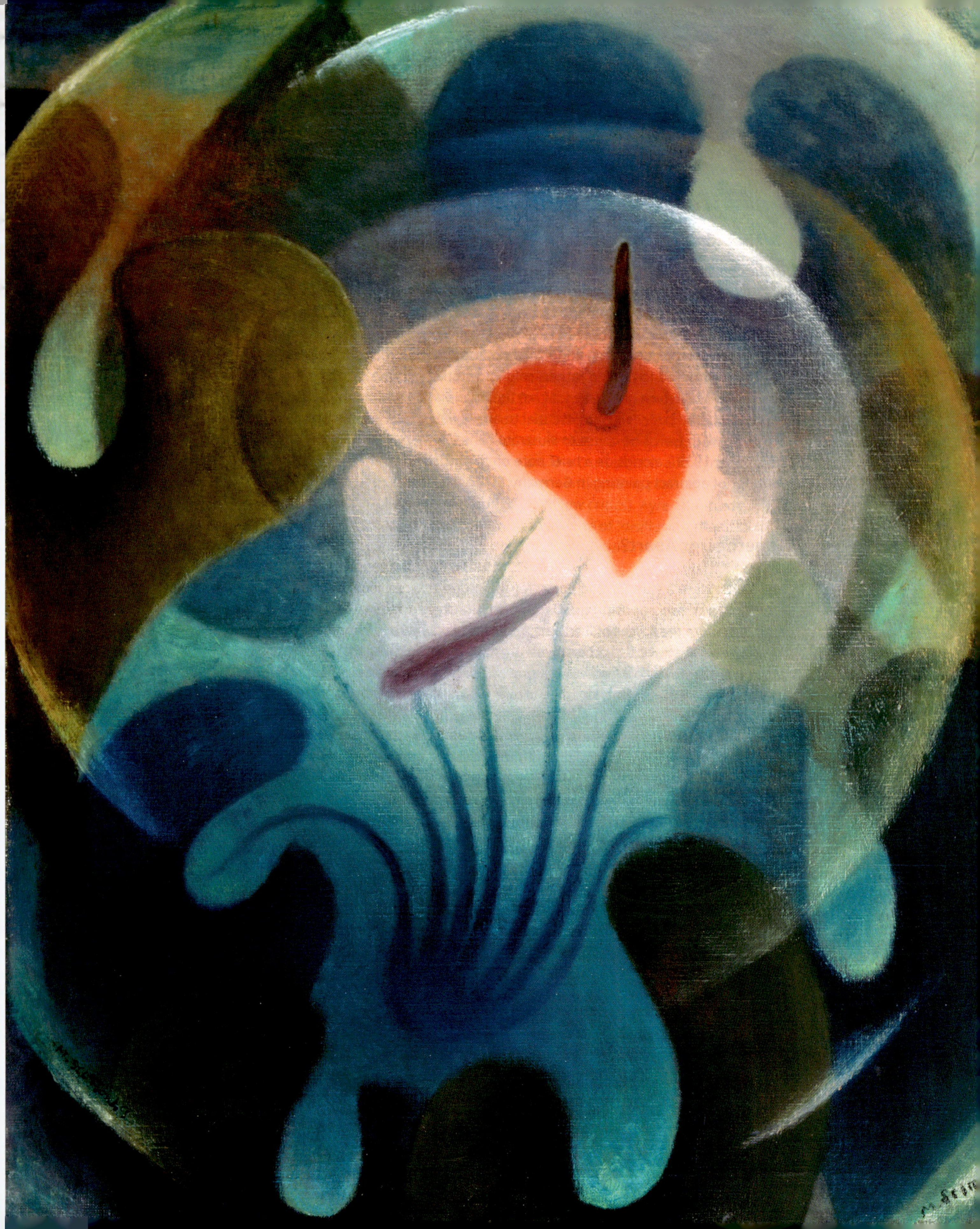

When the Contemporary Arts Society was created, the position of vice-president was filled by Paul-Émile Borduas, who had yet to execute any abstract works. The majority of the founding members, who came for the most part from the anglophone and Jewish communities, belonged to the generation that had begun reshaping modern art during the interwar period.[21] Very soon, however, a growing number of young francophones, frequently from the circles of Pellan and Borduas, began joining the Contemporary Arts Society. Before long, Borduas's group had developed a unified aesthetic position, Automatisme, and its members felt increasingly at odds with the society. In 1946, Claude Gauvreau,[22] adopting his usual confrontational style, expressed the shared position of these young artists in an article titled "Révolution à la Contemporary Arts Society,"[23] which appeared in *Le Quartier Latin* on 3 December. "At last French-Canadian painting exists," he proclaimed as an opener. Unlike anything else, he wrote, it is "aggressive," "disturbing," "new," "absolutely contemporary." It is the art, he maintained, produced by Barbeau (1925–2016), Borduas, Riopelle (1923–2002), Mousseau (1927–1991), Pierre Gauvreau (1922–2011), Roger Fauteux (1923–2021), and Leduc (1916–2014), artists exhibited by the Contemporary Arts Society, a group that had been "conferring its militant name on a crowd of timorous painters who consequently gained the feeling, with little effort, that they were attacking civilization." Gauvreau denounced not only the "timorous" (probably the anglophone figurative painters), but also the artists close to Pellan, such representatives of "academic Fauvism" as Jeanne Rhéaume (1915–2000), Jacques de Tonnancour (1917–2005), and Denyse Gadbois (1921–2013), and "academic Cubists" like Lucien Morin (1918–1998).

Gauvreau's article boldly introduced into the debate an avant-gardist argument based on exclusion and division that heralded the dissolution of the Contemporary Arts Society, by which the Automatistes were feeling increasingly constrained. In 1948, following the society's final exhibition, the members appointed a board of directors composed of Borduas, Marian Dale Scott, Maurice Gagnon, and Luc Choquette. On 12 February, during a meeting of the board, Borduas was elected president, Scott vice-president, and Maurice Gagnon secretary. However, Borduas realized immediately that the board would not support him in the reforms he was planning, and the next day he informed Scott of his decision to resign.[24] This act sounded the death knell of the Contemporary Arts Society, and John Lyman's dream of a united front for living art would not survive the year.

Marian Dale Scott
Anthurium (detail), between 1945 and 1948
ill. 9, page 52

Nor was there any greater unity among the Contemporary Arts Society's francophone members. A few days before Borduas's resignation, on 4 February 1948, Pellan's group had held its first joint exhibition in an annex of the Art Association of Montreal, accompanying the show with a short manifesto, entitled *Prisme d'yeux*. This text by Jacques de Tonnancour, which appeared several months before *Refus global*, asserted the group's openness to all approaches to art and offered a vision of living art echoing that of the 1930s: art must "belong to life." The purity and universality of a work would be assured by its being a "projection of living experience." No doubt in reaction to the Automatiste position, *Prisme d'yeux* denounced all forms of dogmatism and sectarianism. Its signatories, all artists, included painters and sculptors – some figurative some abstract, some Cubist, some Surrealist. The majority were francophone, but there were two anglophones, one of whom was Gordon Webber.[25]

The second and last exhibition presented by the *Prisme d'yeux* group was held at the Tranquille bookstore, from 15 to 29 May 1948. Although their shows attracted some critical attention, the group did not last. There was no stylistic unity among its members, and their manifesto lacked the coherence of the one published by the Automatistes, who would gradually become the francophone art milieu's dominant avant-garde movement. This avant-garde status was due in part to the group's relative aesthetic cohesion (despite individual differences), but it was rooted more importantly in the rhetorical power of *Refus global* and other writings by Borduas and his acolytes – their criticism not only of traditional painting and the conservatism of Quebec society, but also of the rationalism to which they attributed the decadence of Western civilization. It was this that would result in the Automatistes being generally recognized both as Quebec's first abstract artists and as the harbingers of its future "revolutions."

In an essay on the significance of the term abstraction during the 1940s, François-Marc Gagnon mentions an interview with Pellan conducted by Guy Robert, during which the artist expressed regret that he and Borduas had not joined forces in order to "work together toward the evolution of contemporary art." But, as Gagnon aptly points out, "the avant-garde does not add forces, it subtracts them to make way for the new."[26]

In fact, this series of rifts[27] did not put an end to explorations into the complex realm of abstract art, which had clearly not been reduced to the Automatiste vision. Testifying to this were various exhibitions presented during the 1940s and contemporary critical reaction to the work of artists now largely forgotten – including the anglophone artists who are the object of this study. Nevertheless, the separation process was complete. This was made abundantly clear by an event titled "The Meaning of Contemporary Art," organized by the Federation of Canadian Artists and held on 10 January 1949 at the Art Association of Montreal (which would be renamed the Montreal Museum of Fine Arts that same year).

An account of the gathering, which had been advertised in several newspapers, was given by Charles Doyon in *Le Clairon* on 28 January. Among the participants, the critic wrote, "expertly moderated by Professor Scott, the eminent McGill sociologist,"[28] were

> Mr Robert Ayre, of the magazine "Canadian Art," Dr Paul Dumas, a seasoned collector, J.W. Bridges, a professor of anthropology at Sir George Williams College, and Mr Maurice Gagnon the well-known art critic, along with five artists: Messrs Fritz Brandtner and Henry Eveleigh, representing non-figurative painting, Arthur Lismer of the "Group of Seven," Anne Savage, and, representing the "Prisme d'yeux" group, Jacques de Tonnancour.[29]

According to Doyon, "close to five hundred people, attentive and evidently sympathetic, attended the event, at which many different theories on modern art were discussed." And, he added, with a certain irony: "Which means that in Montreal, apart from a few mummified pedants and a handful of young recalcitrants, contemporary painting has won the admiration of an elite. It's a sign of the times when the very serious 'Art Association' responds to it favourably."

The critic then moved on to the question of abstract art: "Some came within a hair's breadth of rejecting abstractionism," he wrote. No doubt wishing to rally the support of his readers, he explained that, to appreciate abstract art, it is necessary to train the eye. In his efforts to convince doubters, however, he employed some rather odd comparisons:

> Abstract painting is like the first oyster, which seems slimy, the first cigarette, which makes you feel sick, the first alcohol, which sends you to sleep ... Pleasure comes with practice, unless one is the angel of abstinence. You need an education, a slow adaptation, essential and intelligent, in the presence of the work of art, if you wish to reach the most subtle levels of emotion.

Although the precise tenor of the discussions is not known, it seems that they tended toward unity rather than division, since Doyon concluded his article with the following words: "Given the marked harmony of this forum's support of contemporary art and of its exchanges, it might be necessary next time to include a few opponents to what is called in fewer and fewer circles 'the anarchy in art.'" This was undoubtedly an allusion to the Automatistes, whom certain conservatives of the time described as anarchists, even Bolsheviks, threatening the very principles of civilization.[30] The "anarchists" were not in fact present at the meeting.

It was noted, finally, that those who spoke in defence of abstraction during the event were two anglophone artists, Brandtner and Eveleigh, who, along with Scott and Webber, had been part of the debates on abstraction taking place during the 1940s. This indicates that "abstraction" was not the sole preserve of francophone artists, but it also serves as a reminder that the anglophones' contribution would be largely eclipsed in the years to come. Part of this forgotten history will be reexplored in the next chapter, in its examination of these artists' work and their critical reception.

Henry Eveleigh
Study for Mother and Child (detail), n.d.
ill. 43, page 96

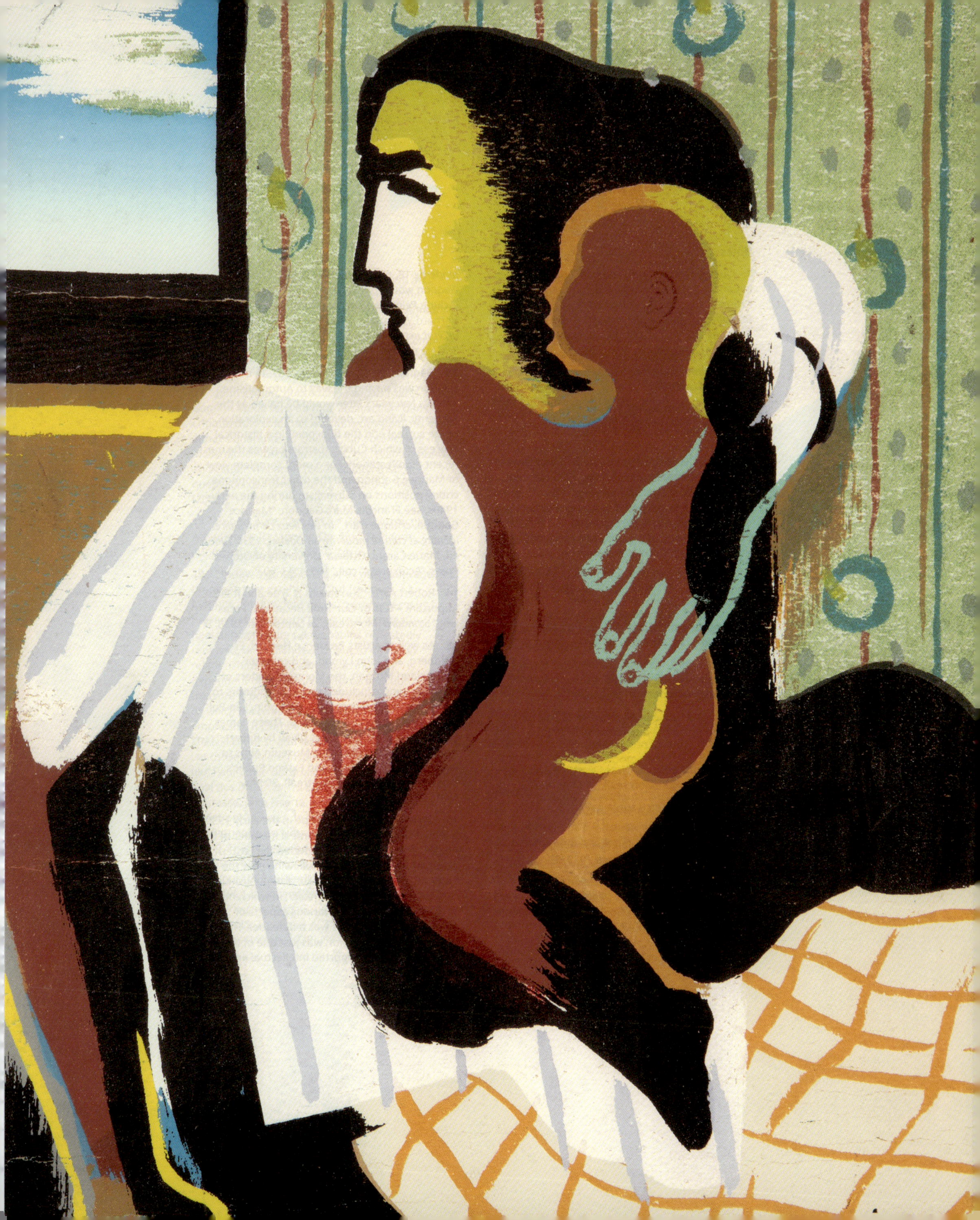

24 François-Marc Gagnon, *Chronique du mouvement automatiste Québécois, 1941–1954* (Montreal: Lanctôt Éditeur, 1998), 453–5.

25 The complete list is as follows: Louis Archambault (1915–2003), Léon Bellefleur (1910–2007), Jacques de Tonnancour (1917–2005), Albert Dumouchel (1916–1971), Gabriel Filion (1920–2005), Pierre Garneau (1926–), Arthur Gladu (1918–1998), Je Anonyme (Jean Benoît, 1922–2010), Lucien Morin (1918–1998), Mimi Parent (1924–2005), Alfred Pellan (1906–1988), Jeanne Rhéaume (1915–2000), Goodridge Roberts (1904–1974), Roland Truchon (1920–1961), and Gordon Webber (1909–1965).

26 Gagnon, "Le sens du mot 'abstraction,'" 131.

27 Borduas's break with the Contemporary Arts Society was actually part of a much broader settling of accounts that would lead to many other rifts, including the one with his friend and colleague at the École du meuble Maurice Gagnon, who had more or less introduced him to Surrealism. But for Borduas, the real war was with Pellan, and it was victory over him and his followers that would allow the Automatistes to lay claim to being Quebec's sole avant-garde movement. The series of Automatiste quarrels would extend to the Communists and even to the French Surrealists, whom Borduas judged to still be tainted with traces of the objective world, even if their referents operated within a space of dreams and the subconscious. See Marcel Saint-Pierre, *Une abstention coupable: enjeux politiques du manifeste Refus global* (Montreal: M éditeur, 2013).

28 In fact, the lawyer, poet, and social-democratic activist Frank (Francis Reginald) Scott was a professor in McGill University's law faculty.

29 Charles Doyon, "Débats et expositions," *Le Clairon* (Saint-Hyacinthe), 28 January 1949, 5. The second part of the article discusses recent exhibitions by Marcelle Ferron and Marian Dale Scott.

30 See Dominique Laberge, *Anarchie dans l'art* (Montreal: Éditions Fernand Pilon, 1945); and René Bergeron, *Art et bolchevisme* (Montreal: Fides, 1946).

Gordon Webber
Design No. 1, Vermont (detail), 1946
ill. 64, page 126

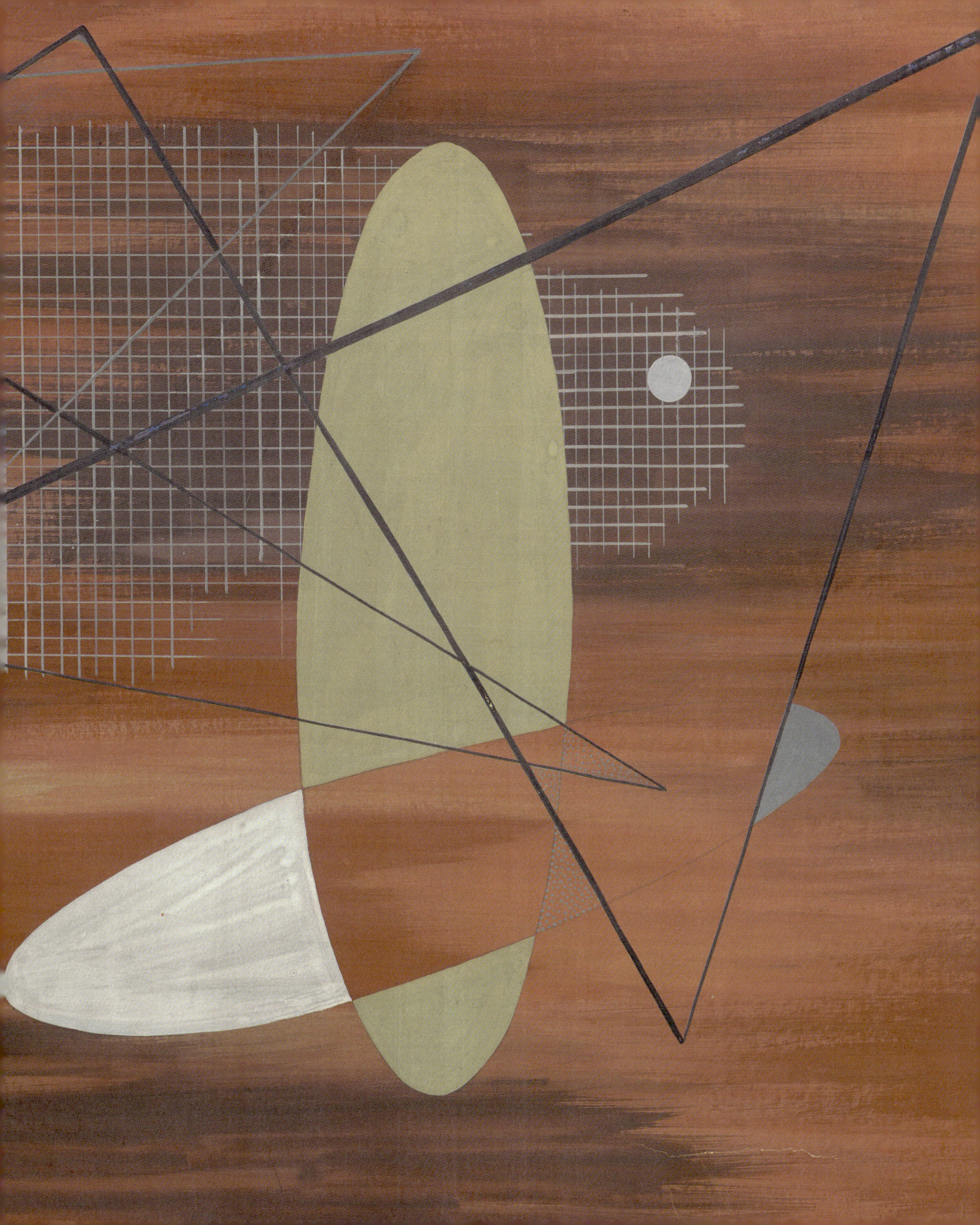

CHAPTER 2

The Polysemy of Abstraction

In 1930s Montreal, before the exhibition *Art of Our Day* put modern European works – including several abstractions by Wassily Kandinsky – on public view in 1939, scarcely any non-figurative paintings had been shown in the city, aside, possibly, from a few Brandtners. As we have seen, the notion of abstraction was rarely discussed by critics, except in a handful of articles published by Robert Ayre toward the end of the decade and in the writings of Maurice Gagnon, who saw the phenomenon as an "excess of abstract thinking" arising from Cubism.[1]

Alfred Pellan's return from Europe and the retrospective of his work shown in Quebec City and Montreal in 1940 attracted considerable media attention. In the exhibition catalogue, Pellan divided his works into three categories: figurative paintings, non-figurative decorative works and sketches, and finally drawings, gouaches, watercolours, and posters. The exhibition not only established Pellan as a major figure of modern art in Quebec, it also sparked a debate on the meaning of abstraction, often associated with Surrealism and Cubism. François-Marc Gagnon, who explored the sense given to the word abstraction during the 1940s in some depth, particularly in relation to the Pellan-Borduas clash, showed how, following Pellan's exhibition, it became fashionable among critics to employ the term. They nevertheless vacillated, he explained, between two viewpoints: either abstraction was entirely non-representational and consisted of nothing but interplays of form and colour, or it represented something, but not anything in the external world. In the latter case, it was the artist's self – their inner world, their dreams, their desires – that was projected onto the canvas.[2]

Borduas, keen to distinguish himself from Pellan, felt obliged to take a stand on the notion of abstraction, now associated in the critical discourse with his rival. Consequently, as François-Marc Gagnon has shown, Borduas and his supporters would defend the view that abstract art, like Cubism, had become academic, an outdated form of artistic expression. Borduas entirely assimilated an idea suggested to him by François Hertel[3] in a letter dated 13 December 1941: "The true Pellan is abstract. The true Borduas is concrete."[4]

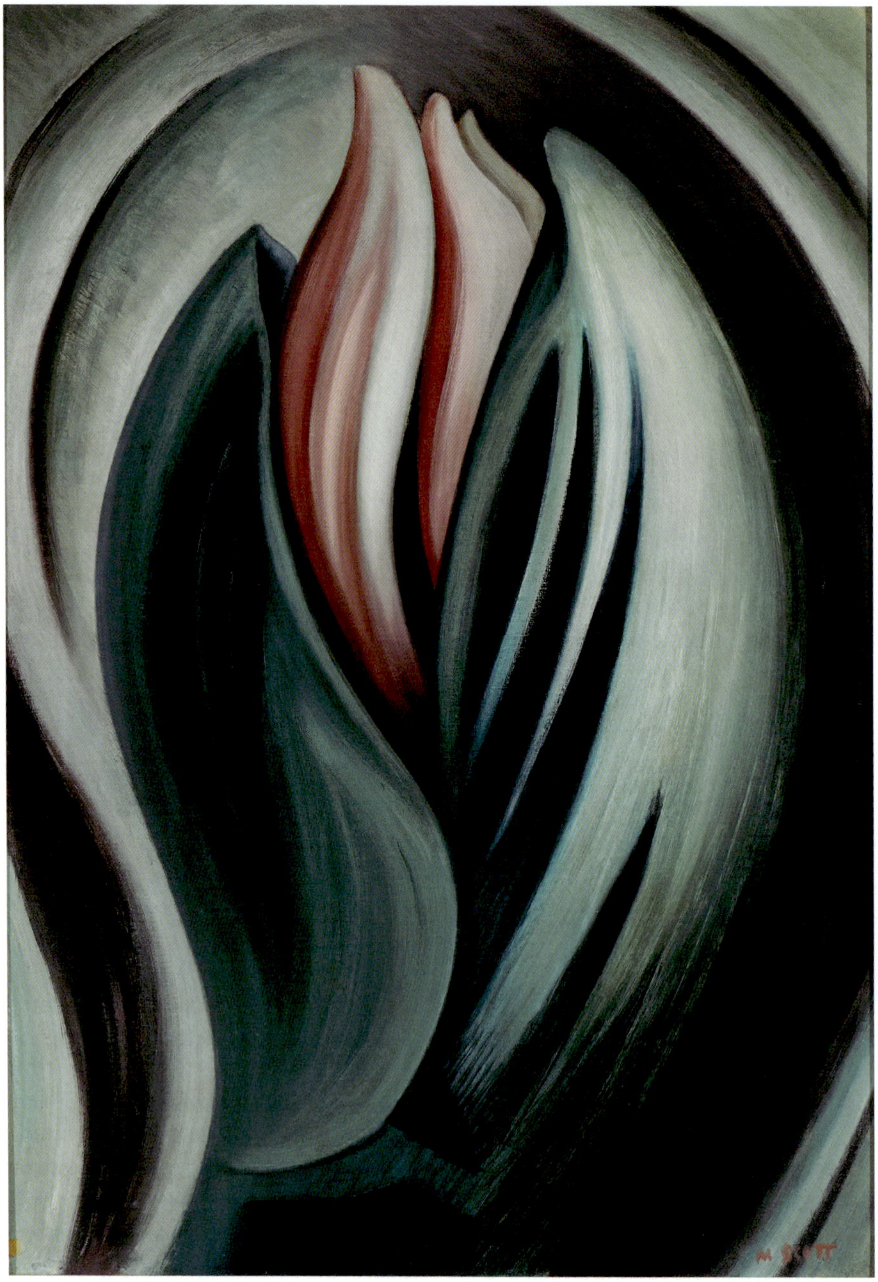

ill. 5 (*above*)
Marian Dale Scott
Bud, about 1939

ill. 7 (*opposite*)
Marian Dale Scott
Fire Escape, 1939

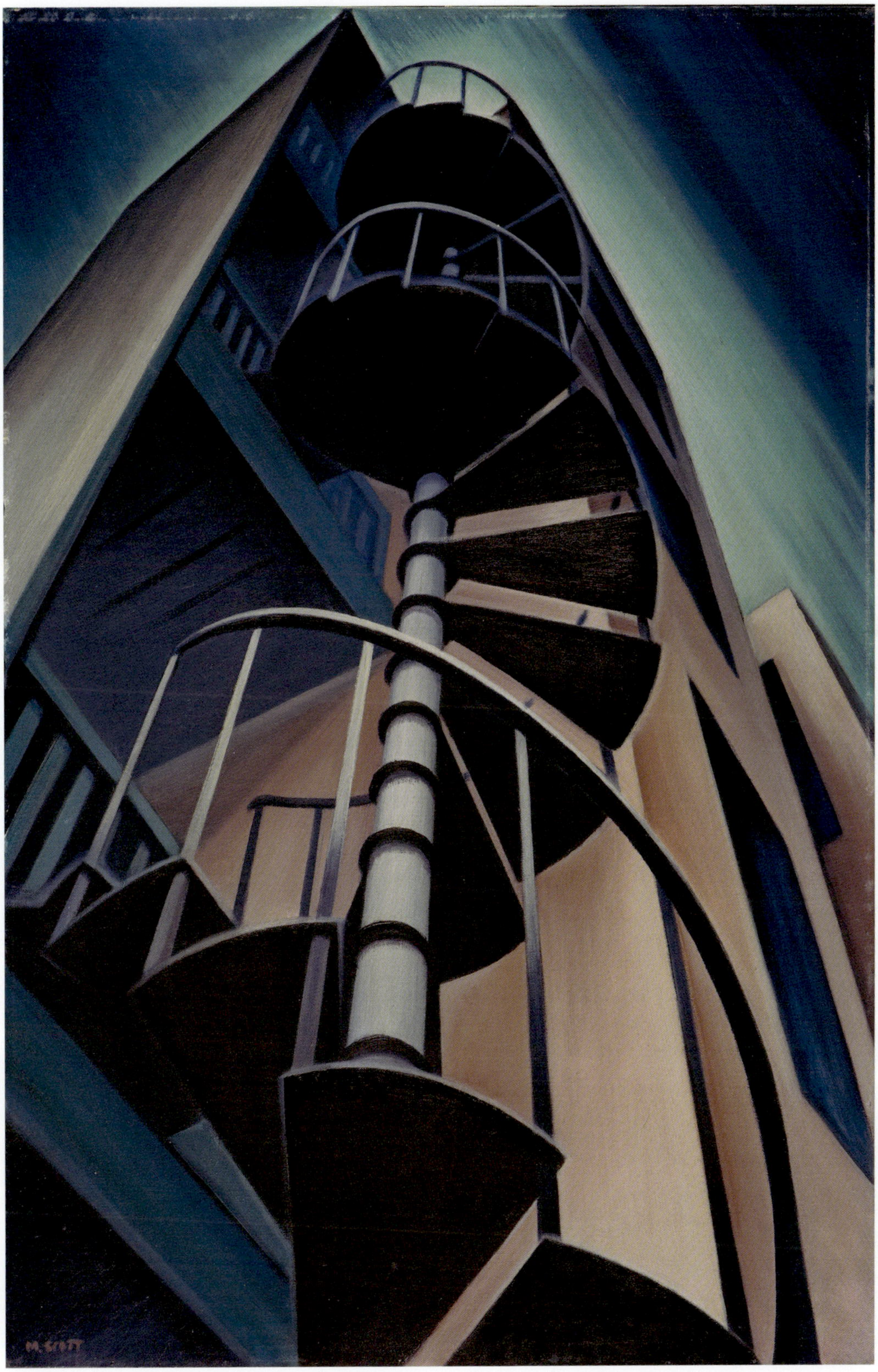
M. SCOTT

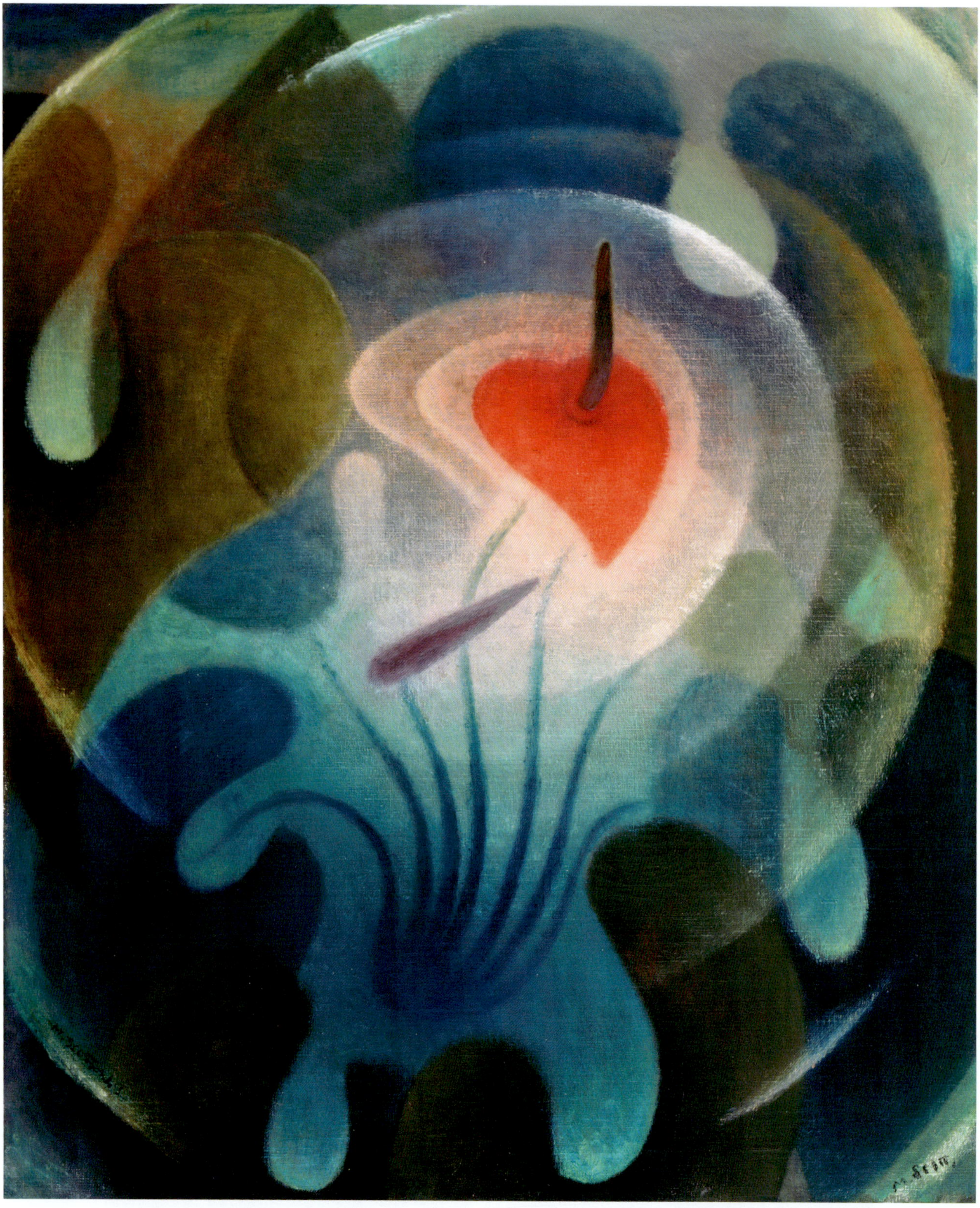

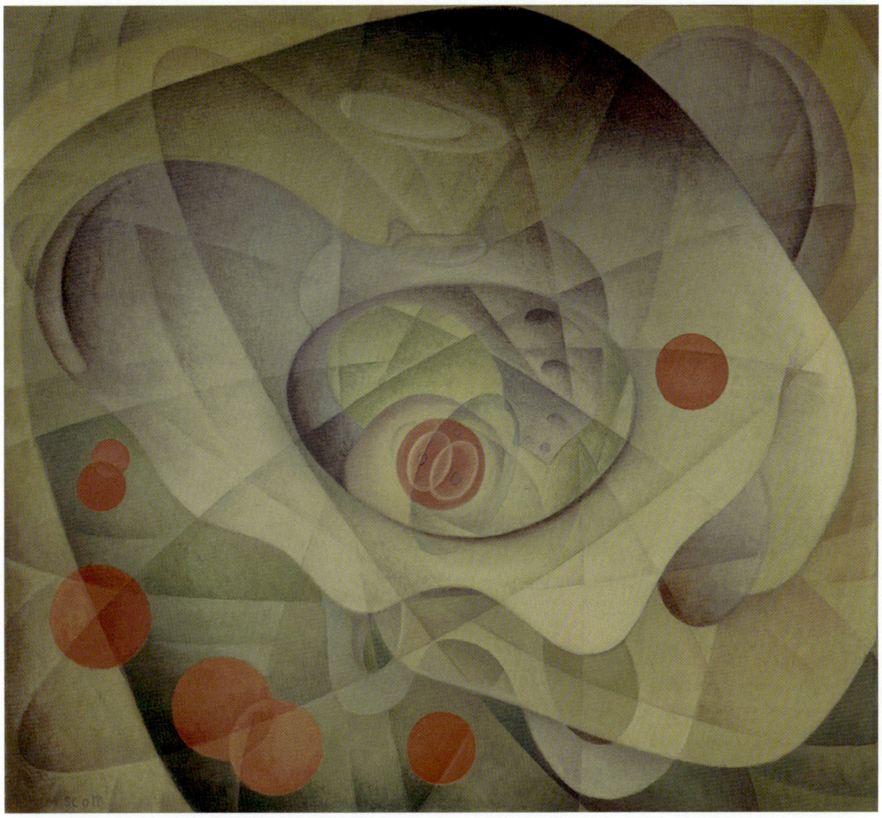

The 1940s: The Sources of Life and Evolution

This formal approach, characteristic of Scott's work from the 1930s and aimed at the creation of a "significant" art through the casting of a critical gaze over the contemporary world, would shift into a new vision in the following decade. In the fall of 1941, Hans Selye, at that time an assistant professor of histology at McGill University, commissioned the artist to execute a mural on the theme of endocrinology to adorn a lecture hall at the university. By way of preparation, Scott researched the subject in some depth, discovering in the process an entirely new visual world – the microscopic world of cells and atoms, the fundamental structures of life.

The mural (ill. 90), unveiled on 26 June 1943, would mark the start of a new phase in Scott's oeuvre. Henceforth, her search for significance would focus on reproduction in the living world, and on the principles of growth and evolution. Her manner altered.

ill. 9 (*opposite*)
Marian Dale Scott
Anthurium, between 1945 and 1948

ill. 8 (*above*)
Marian Dale Scott
Atom, Bone, and Embryo, 1943

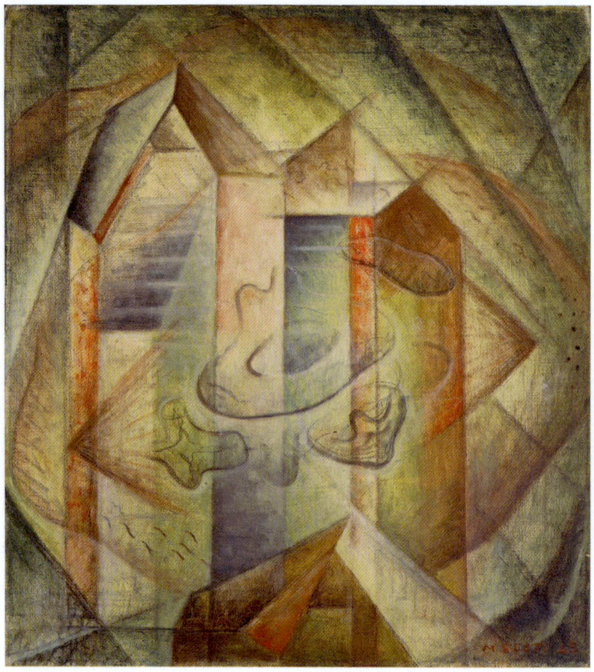

> With the change of subject matter of my painting I see change of style. While my painting was mainly concerned with man's control of nature, painting fitted by being angular and rigidly geometric … Now that my concern is organic growth my way will become more fluid, still delicately precise but less geometric, less static.[15]

The new paintings also revealed a more evidently feminine facet of her work. On 1 December 1943, while executing the *Atom, Bone, and Embryo* series, Scott noted in her diary that she wanted it to be "delicate, feminine, but sure and strong."

This feminine approach to the organic world echoed the artist's style in the flower paintings of the preceding decade. This was a theme that she still occasionally returned to, moreover, as witness *Anthurium*, which combines a floral motif and a series of cell-like forms in a composition whose superimpositions and transparencies link it directly to the works inspired by the biological realm.

ill. 10
Marian Dale Scott
Cell and Crystal, 1945

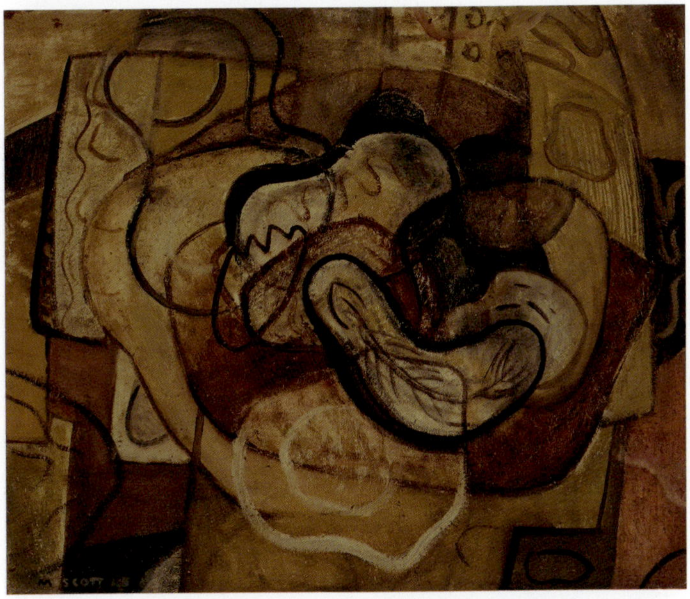

Superficially, at least, Scott's exploration of the cellular world seems to align her with the major trend in contemporary art known as biomorphism. During the 1920s, 1930s, and 1940s, cellular, protoplasmic, and biomorphic forms would inspire a good many artists and designers.[16] But the circumstances of production varied from one creator to another and, in Scott's case, her use of such forms was integral to a philosophical meditation on the significance of evolution in the living world.

In 1945, alongside the cellular forms, new motifs began appearing in Scott's images, such as crystals (ill. 10) and fossils (ill. 11). Tightly interwoven within the pictorial space, these elements expanded the scope of the artist's preoccupation with time and evolution and rendered her efforts to transpose it onto canvas more complex. On 18 September 1946, she wrote in her diary that these works fused "the formed and the unformed ... the done and the becoming." In the introduction to her 1954 solo show at the Dominion Gallery, she discussed one of the paintings

ill. 11
Marian Dale Scott
Cells and Fossils (Variations on a Theme), 1945

work, wrote that, like Georgia O'Keeffe and Barbara Hepworth, who were "among those who had denied their 'femininity' to confront the problems of creation," she was deliberately sacrificing "the decorative charm which is the heritage of most women painters, to reach after true realization."[19]

Scott's production of the 1940s was often identified with abstraction. In 1948, she exhibited four works in a Canadian Group of Painters exhibition that included *Cell and Crystal*. In his review of the show, the critic Andrew Bell described the abstract works on view as "the life-blood of a living art" and evidence of their creators' search for a language adapted to the new and still strange realities of the scientific age. Speaking specifically of Scott's works, he declared that her research into the secrets of life had produced results that were both "mature and provocative."[20]

It should come as no surprise, on the other hand, that Claude Gauvreau, an ardent defender of Automatisme, was not impressed by Scott's abstractions. Speaking of those she showed with the Contemporary Arts Society in 1946, he wrote:

> Marian Scott is exhibiting a couple of her systematically conceived and systematically executed abstractions on a given theme ... This is slick painting, which is bound to be immensely popular. But why are some critics, who strangely accuse Barbeau and Riopelle of always doing the same thing, in ecstasies over these endless reiterations, which have become so boringly repetitive?[21]

However, two years later, in 1948, on the occasion of a Canadian Group of Painters exhibition whose participants he divided into two groups – the "generous explorers" and the "exploiters" – he had moderated his judgement of Scott, who, with Goodridge Roberts, was one of the few artists to find favour in his eyes. With her painting *Fossils*, Gauvreau wrote, she was "on the point of succumbing to spontaneity," although she was still hovering at the frontier of "abstract Cubism."[22]

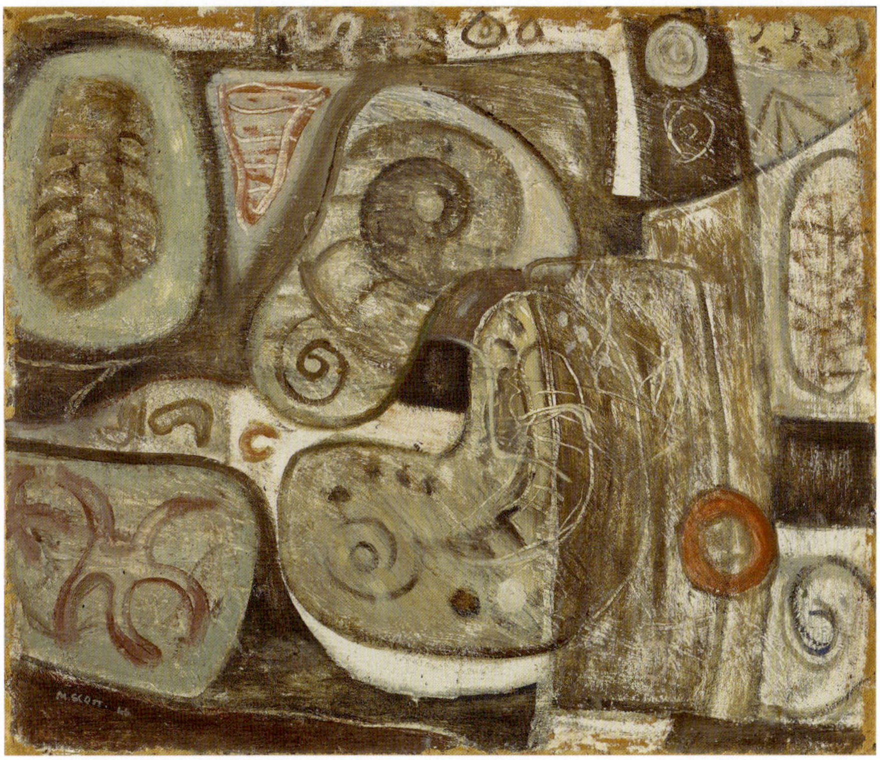

ill. 14
Marian Dale Scott
Fossils, 1946

For the Automatistes, as we have seen, Cubism, so often associated with abstraction, was the final manifestation of rational painting, whose demise was the inevitable outcome of the Automatiste exploration of the surreal.

Two exhibitions held in 1949 prompted further comments about Scott's relationship to abstraction. The first was the exhibition *Marian Scott and Gordon Webber*, presented in January at the Gallery XII of the Art Association of Montreal (which would become the Montreal Museum of Fine Arts during that same year),[23] concurrently with the Canadian Group of Painters' annual exhibition; the second was the exhibition *How to Appreciate a Work of Art*, held at the Montreal Museum of Fine Arts in October.

The Scott-Webber exhibition gave rise to a number of reviews whose authors, disconcerted by the radical non-objectivity of Webber's paintings and, in some cases, by its "geometric coldness," questioned the meaning of the works. We shall return to these reactions later. As far as Scott was concerned, the critic for the *Montreal Daily Star* found the meaning of *Stone and Protoplasm* (of which the artist exhibited several versions) impossible to fathom.[24] But Charles Hamel, writing in *Le Canada*, maintained that, rather than wondering about the meaning, it was perhaps best to appreciate the "visual pleasure":

> What Marian Scott is striving to represent in her painting, we've been told, is the eternal battle between life and death ... This is perhaps not immediately obvious when one looks at her painting, but on the other hand her sophisticated approach provides an aesthetic pleasure that can be enjoyed without speculating about all sorts of hidden meanings.[25]

Finally, while Renée Normand of *Le Canada* was far from enthusiastic about the "geometric system" of Gordon Webber's canvases, which she described as "non-figurative, 'abstract' in the simplest sense of the word," she liked Marian Scott's approach, in which abstraction retained a few figurative referents and revolved around a philosophical reflection:

> After those by Mr Webber, it was a pleasure to see paintings that, although non-figurative, still remain highly plastic. In Mrs Scott's works, the interplay, rhythm and proportions of the forms are handled harmoniously. This pleasant painting, neither fish nor fowl, marshals abstract and representational elements in a highly decorative manner, showing a refined style and considerable technical assurance. Moreover, Mrs Scott is the only Canadian painter of her kind who knows exactly why she paints like she does while remaining logical in her conclusions. It's a great quality.[26]

Taken together, the reviews reflect the difficulties encountered by the critics, and no doubt by the public too, when it came to thinking about abstraction. This general incomprehension was likely what prompted the Montreal Museum of Fine Arts to present, as part of a Université de Montréal seminar offered by Professor L.V. Randall, *How to Appreciate a Work of Art.* On view from 12 to 30 October 1949, this didactic show was composed of a selection of original works and reproductions designed to introduce visitors to the analysis and appreciation of modern art by offering them a circuit that ran from figurative to abstract works, including paintings by Borduas, Scott, and Webber. The abstractions impressed the critic Roland Chauvin to varying degrees. Writing in *Le Quartier Latin*, he seemed quite unconcerned by the question of "meaning" and was evidently particularly struck by Borduas's contribution, in which he saw "nothing evoking objective reality" but that he judged to be "a brilliant, virtually inexhaustible composition."[27]

The 1950s: From Interrelations to Non-objectivity

During the 1950s, when critics and public alike were being confronted by a growing number of abstract trends that took increasingly diverse forms, including post-Automatisme and the Plasticien movement, Scott's work remained on the fringes: it was through an abstraction still partially based on references to the tangible world that she strove to convey her philosophical reflections. Compared to her earlier production, however, the paintings from the 1950s display greater gestural freedom and a more marked preoccupation with effects of texture and

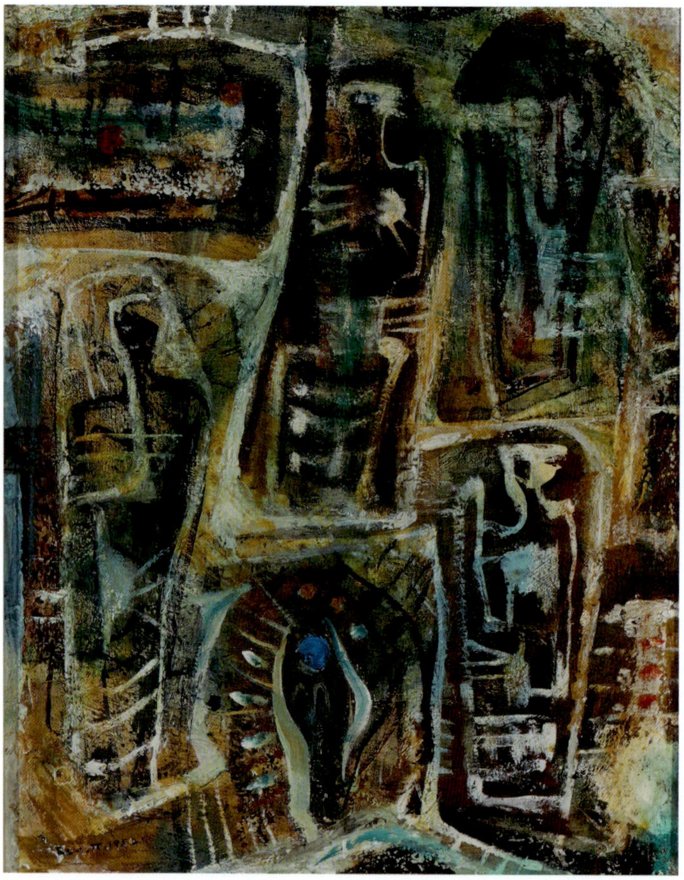

matière. She also began drawing on new cultural sources, including Christian art. Icons, stained-glass windows, and figures echoing the rowed statues that adorn the façades of Gothic cathedrals would supplant the motifs inspired by "ancestral" art, giving rise to such series as *Façades*, *Iconic*, and *Apostles.* According to the critic Charles Doyon, the *Apostles* – often depicted in their cathedral niches (ill. 17) – "are simply there for visual reasons. They are the pretext for a row of vertical forms that expresses the idea of assembly."[28]

ill. 15
Marian Dale Scott
Façade No. 2, 1954

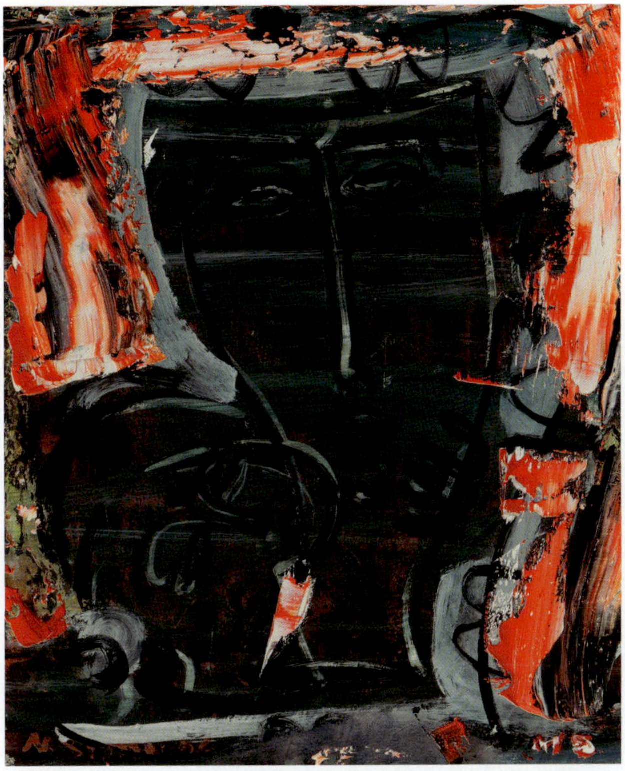

In fact, as Scott explained several times in writing, the use of motifs drawn from religious art was part of a meditation on the complexity of human interrelations that had begun early in the decade with the *Groups* series. She had embarked on the series after seeing an exhibition held at the Montreal Museum of Fine Arts in January 1952 that included a number of prints by the British artist Henry Moore. Speaking of *Groups*, the artist wrote: "Precarious integration. Individual figures but part of a larger whole: separate but interrelated. Impressions of inner as well as of outer structure."[29] These musings on the notion of separation, the interrelations between human beings, and their confinement within internal and external structures can be applied both to the individuals depicted in public spaces and to the religious figures isolated in their niches.

ill. 16
Marian Dale Scott
Iconic, about 1955

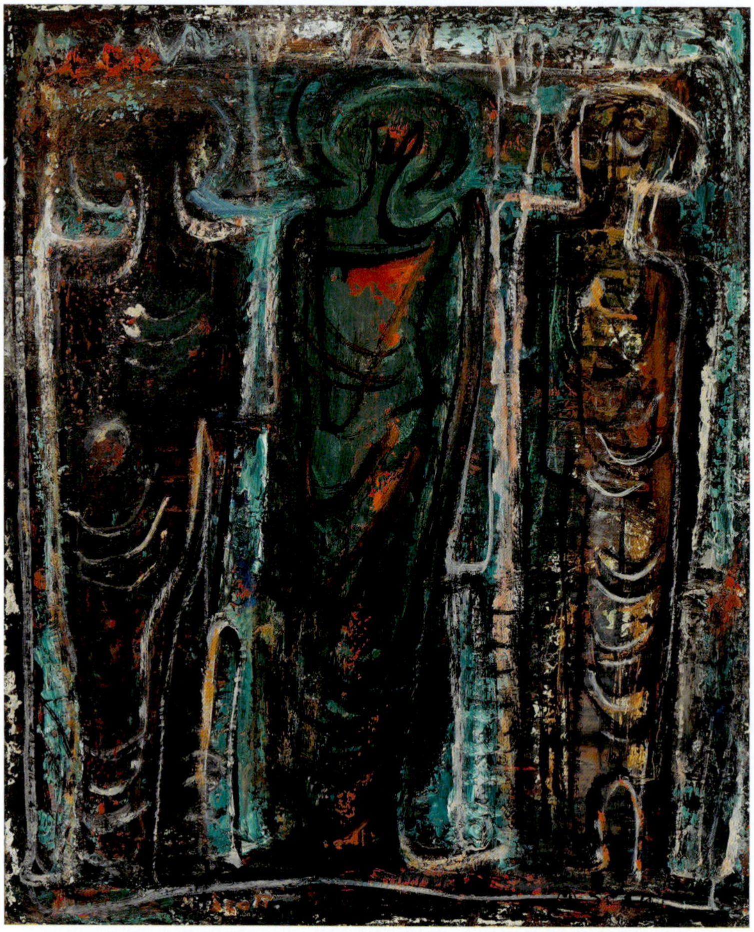

ill. 17 (*above*)
Marian Dale Scott
Façade No. 6, about 1955

ill. 18 (*opposite*)
Marian Dale Scott
Group No. 10, 1952

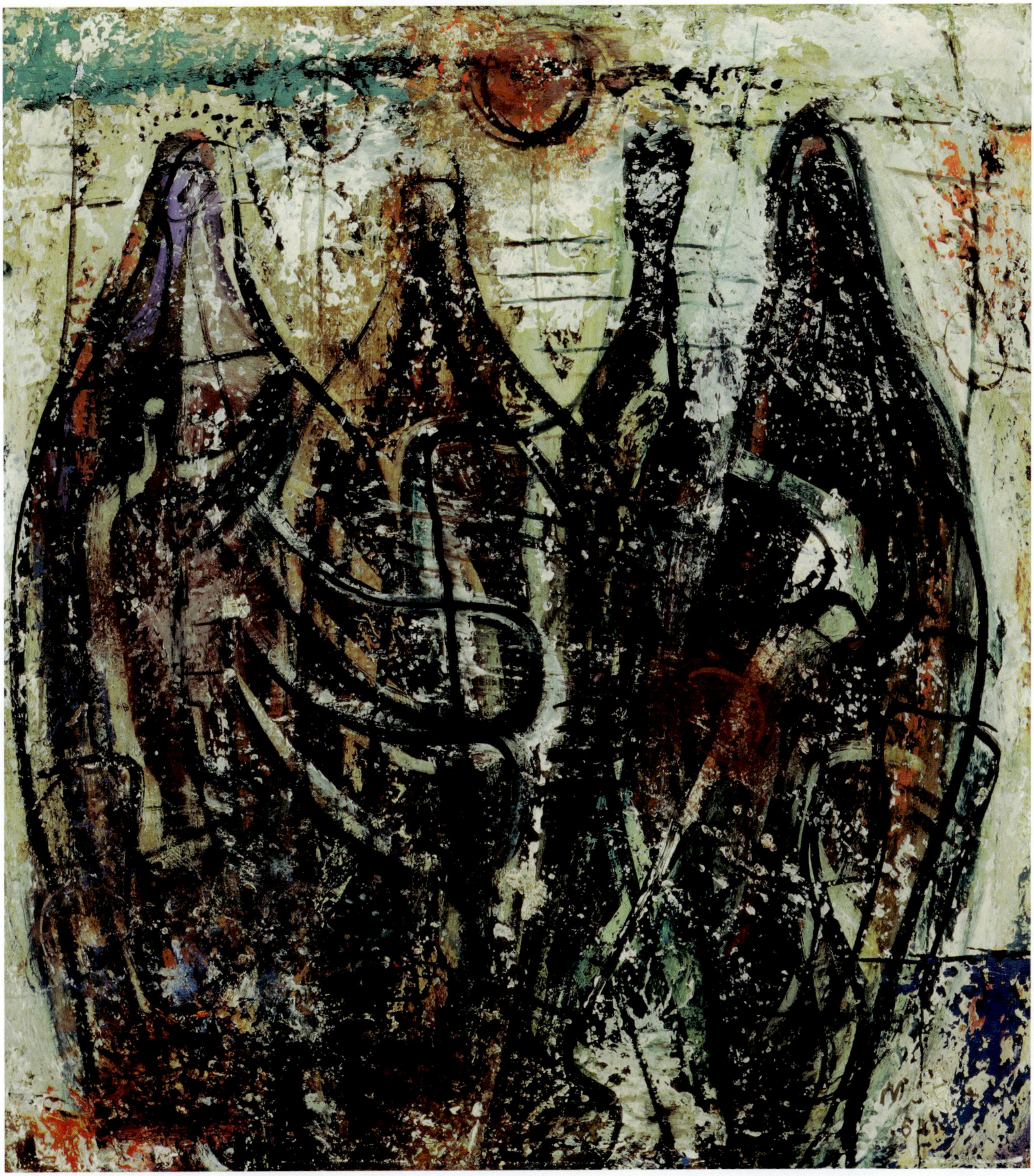

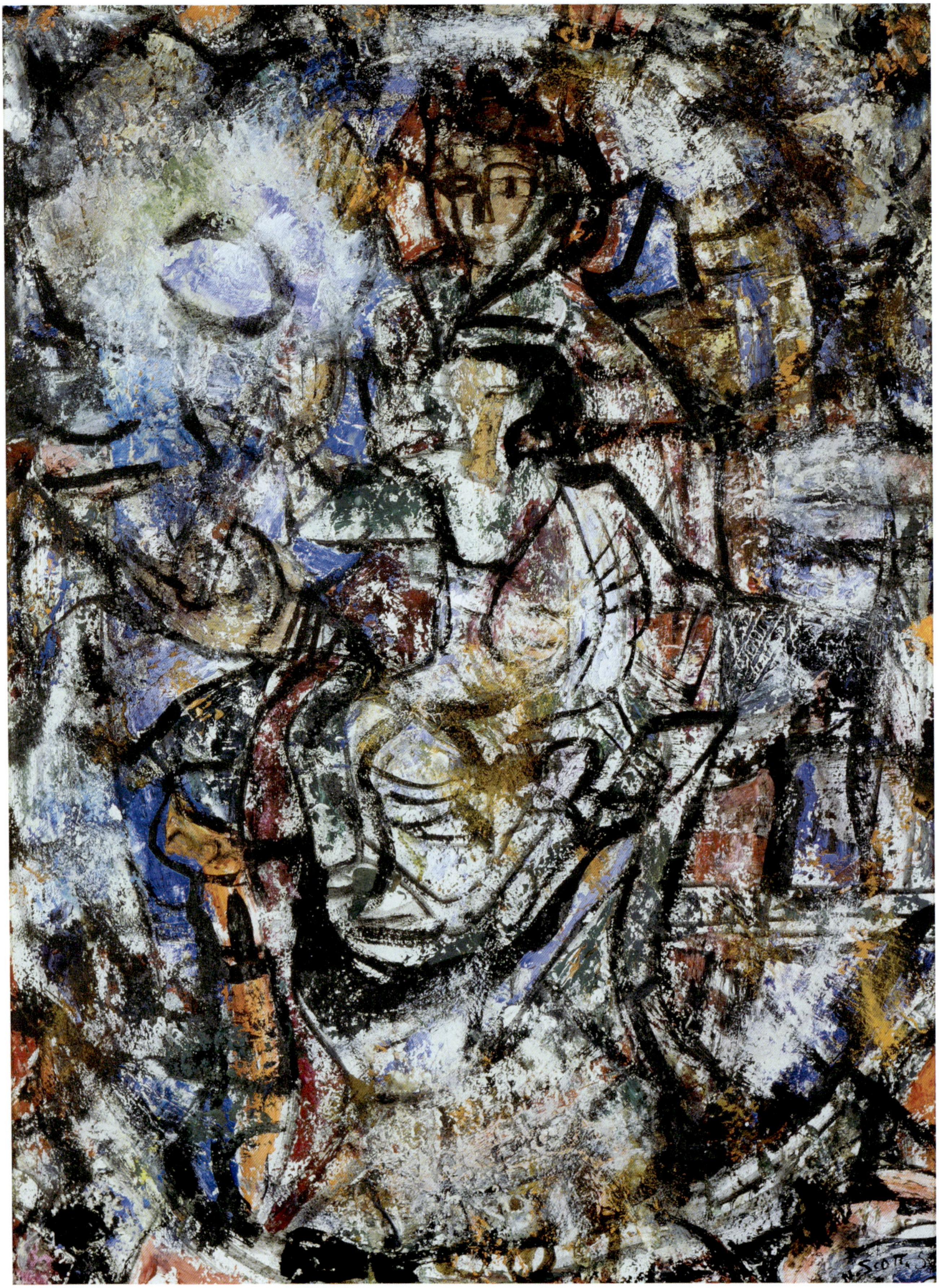

From the mid-1950s, however, new stylistic influences would be revealed in paintings like *Translation (Iconic) No. 1*, which, with its expressively gestural lines and spontaneously applied areas of colour, has a more "American" feel. Scott was well informed about developments on the New York art scene.[30] The critic Rodolphe de Repentigny took note of the artist's change of direction, and, in the fall of 1956, reviewing her exhibition of forty-seven works at the Dominion Gallery, which included *Translation (Iconic) No. 1*, he wrote:

> The exhibition actually shows proof of far greater audacity than we are used to seeing from our painters. There is quite a distance between the [Henry] Mooresque drawings in earth colours and black of the "Facades" and the dazzling "Translations," whose blues and vivid reds unfurl across brilliant whites ... It is hard to avoid seeing here a more or less direct influence of American painting gradually replacing a more British romanticism.[31]

Following Scott's 1958 exhibition at the Dominion Gallery, in which she showed a number of recent works, including several from the *Figures* series, Rodolphe de Repentigny declared that the artist's visual universe was now comparable to that of De Kooning, Pollock, and Tobey.[32] Robert Ayre also perceived the affiliation with American Abstract Expressionism but was less willing to accompany Scott on the path she was taking toward non-figurative art. His review of the 1958 show makes his reservations concerning her new work very clear:

> Mrs. Scott's painting has implications of significance that I have felt to be religious in a deeply mystical way, a search, a pilgrimage, that is more than an exploration of the possibilities of painting for its own sake. She has remained figurative, though her figures be hieroglyphic, but in her new work she has become increasingly abstract and, in my understanding, more cryptical. Whether the figures be single, or in couples, or the theme be "Community," they are lost in a dense maze. As they become blurred, written over by the white writing of Tobey or blotted out by Pollock drippings and spatters, I, too, am lost. I accept the seriousness of her intentions in these themes and variations, but she has gone where I cannot follow.[33]

ill. 19
Marian Dale Scott
Translation (Iconic) No. 1, 1955

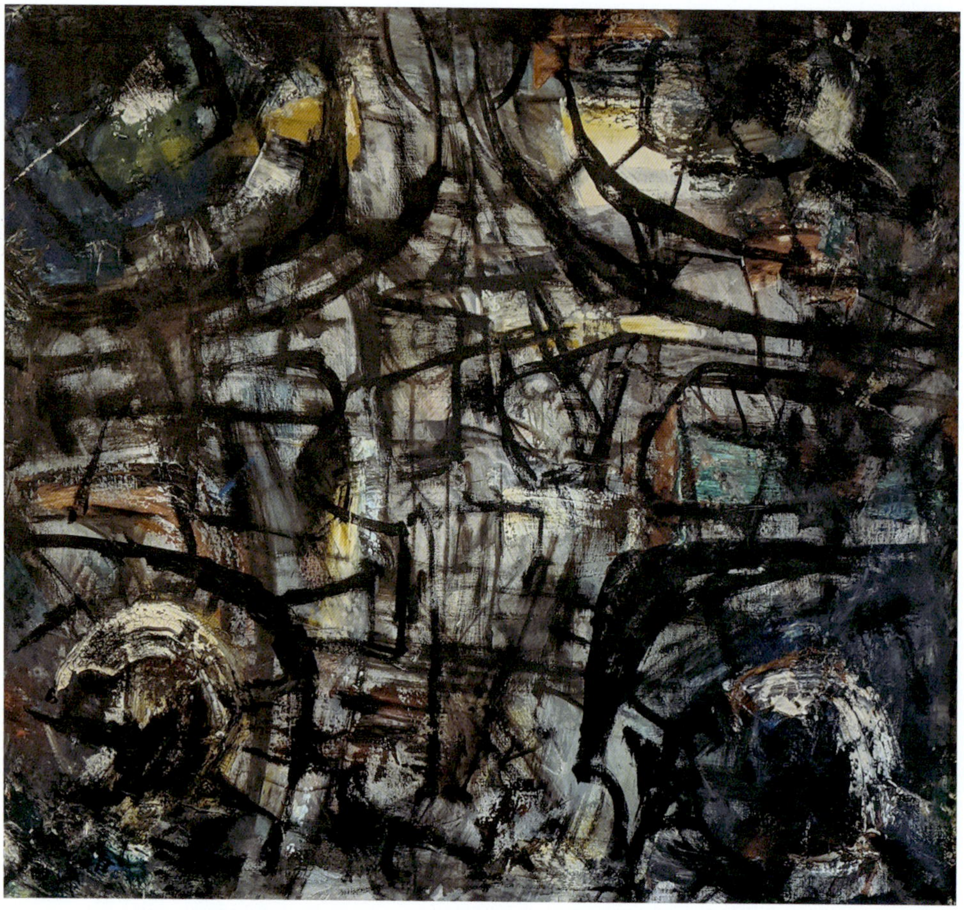

ill. 20
Marian Dale Scott
Figure No. 2, about 1957

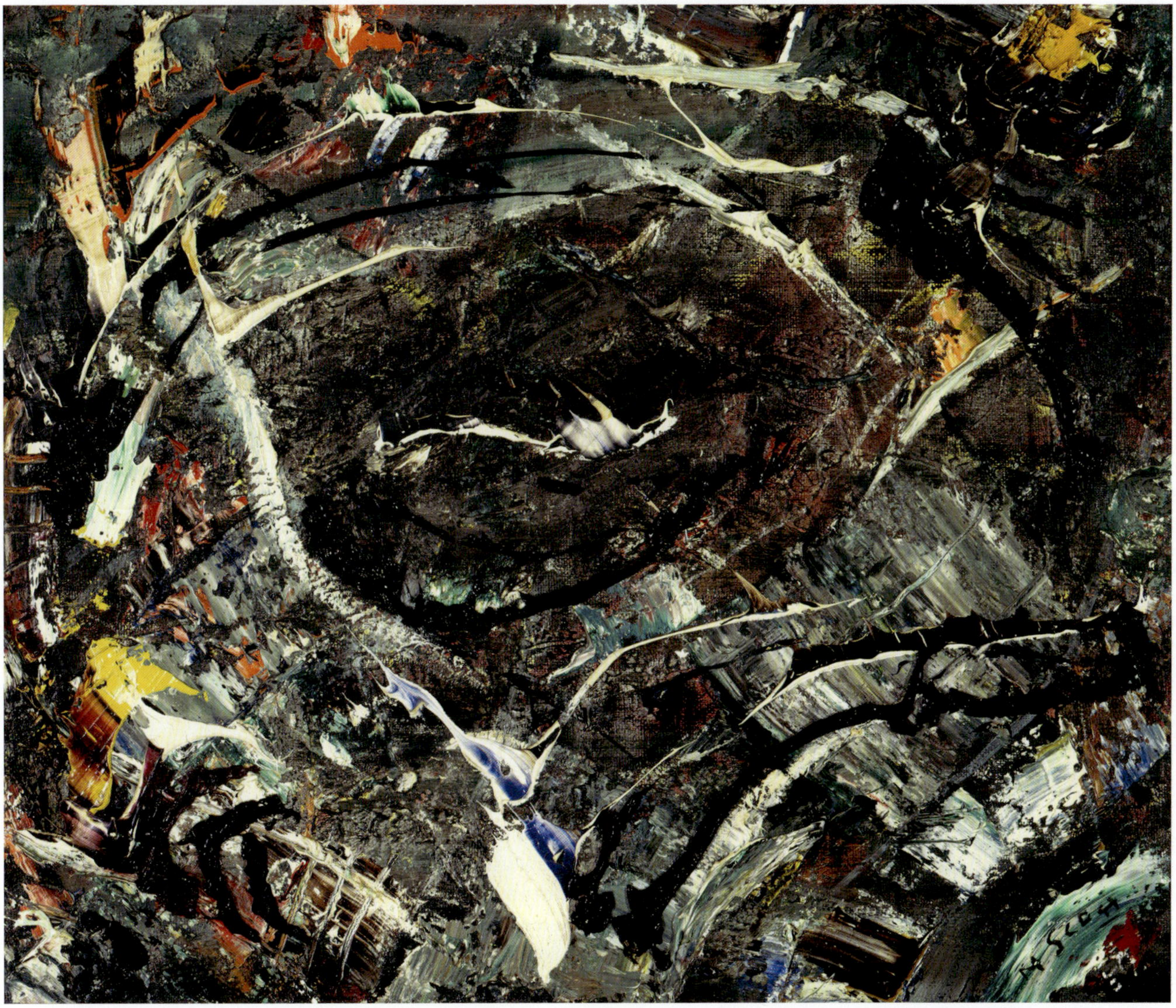

ill. 21
Marian Dale Scott
Out of the Night, about 1959

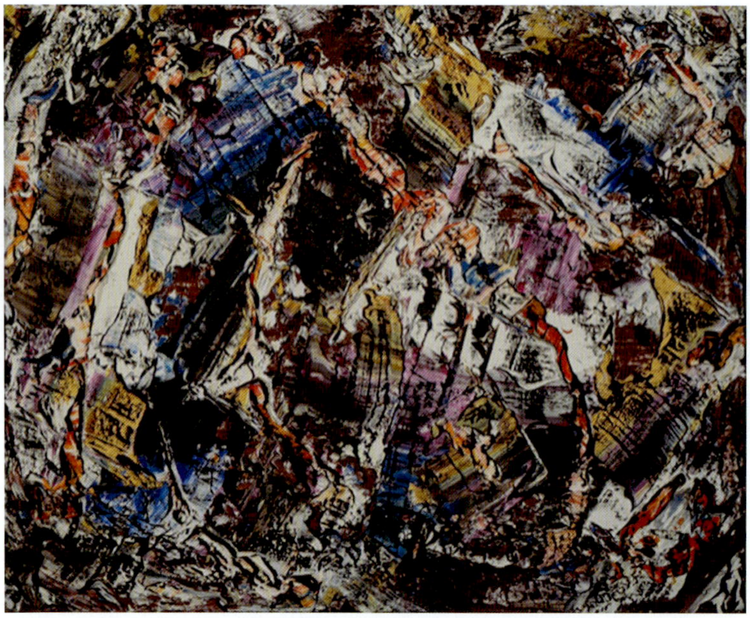

Marian Dale Scott was unquestionably moving closer to non-objective abstraction. In an interview she gave to *The Montrealer* in June 1958, she declared: "As I get older, I wish more and more that my paintings speak for themselves. I like to paint with as much of me as possible."[34] Between 1958 and 1961, her approach developed into a form of purely gestural abstraction (ills. 21 and 22) that she described as "transitional." This would lead into a period dominated by a geometric abstraction that occasionally encompassed a certain fluidity of line – as in the 1966 work *Untitled*, which belongs to the Musée d'art de Joliette. Her diary indicates that her reading included such authors as the formalist critic Clement Greenberg and the radical philosopher Herbert Marcuse, who believed that non-objective art was a "way to liberation."[35] Scott's permanent shift into pure abstraction would do nothing to alter the critical and political sensibility she would retain until the end of her life.

ill. 22
Marian Dale Scott
Out of the Night No. 2, about 1959

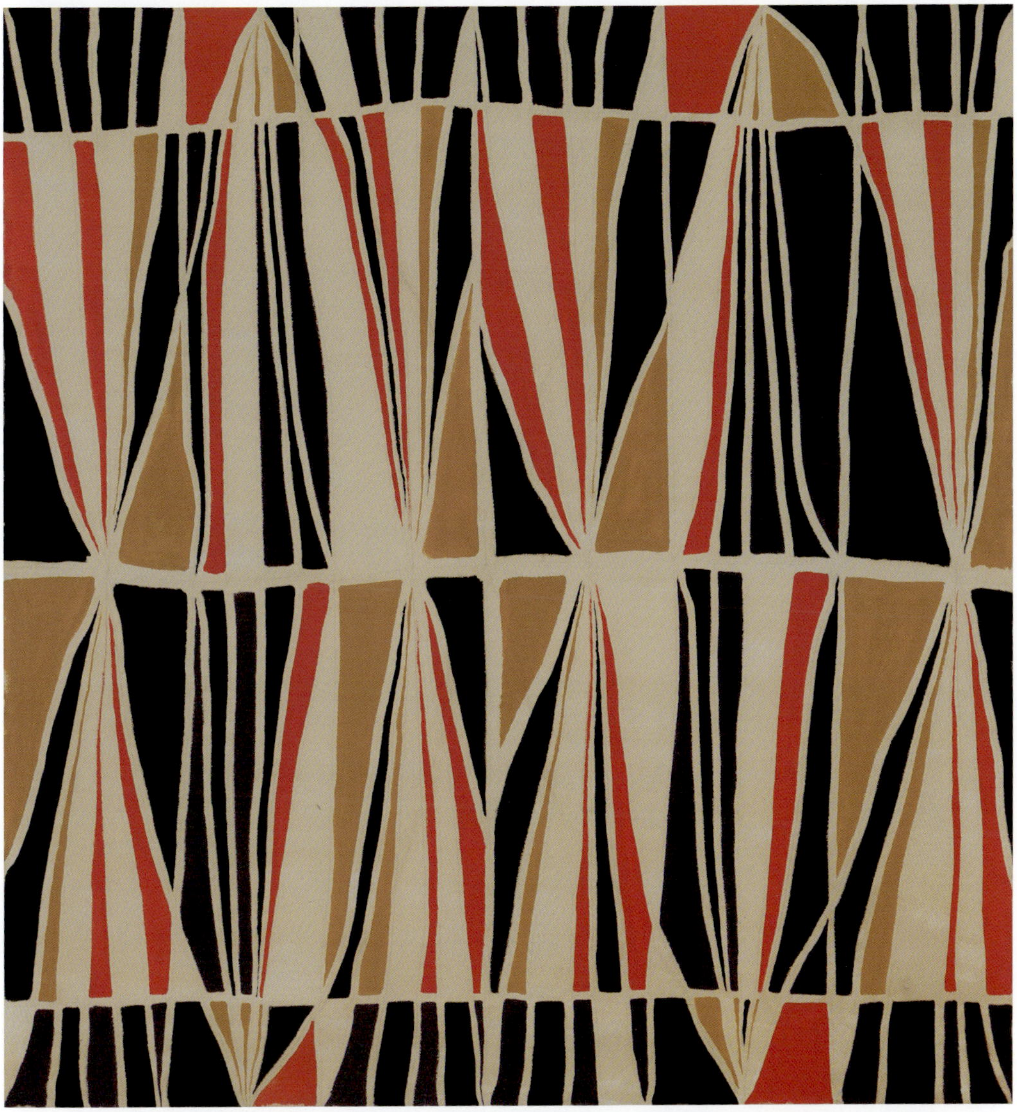

ill. 23
Marian Dale Scott
Untitled, 1966

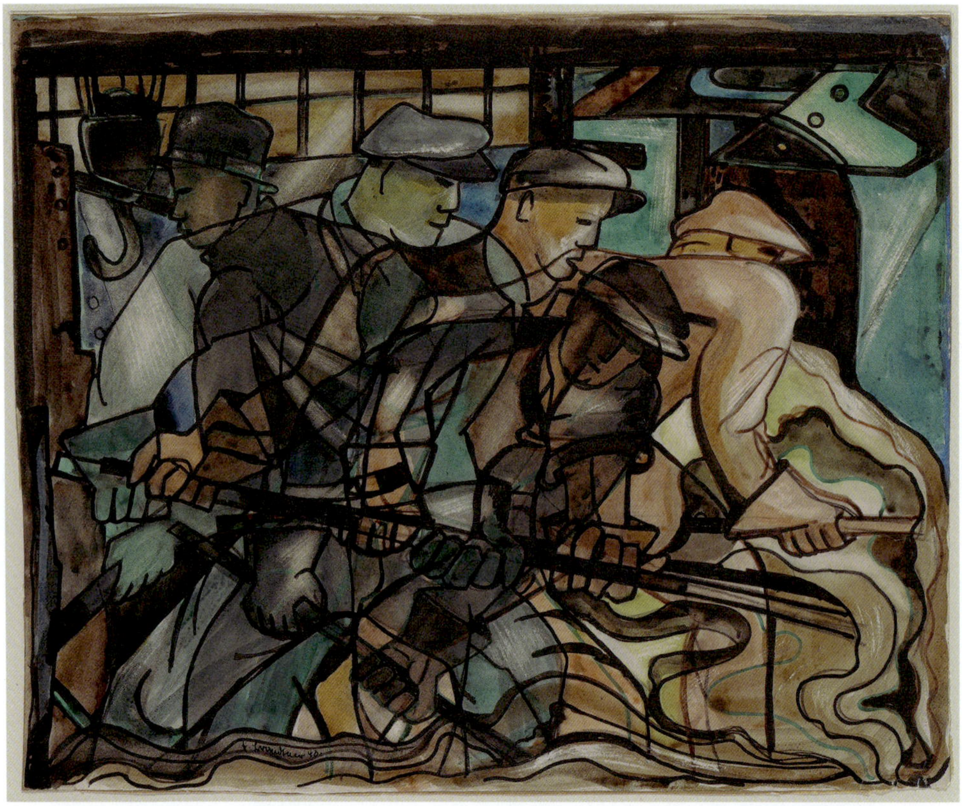

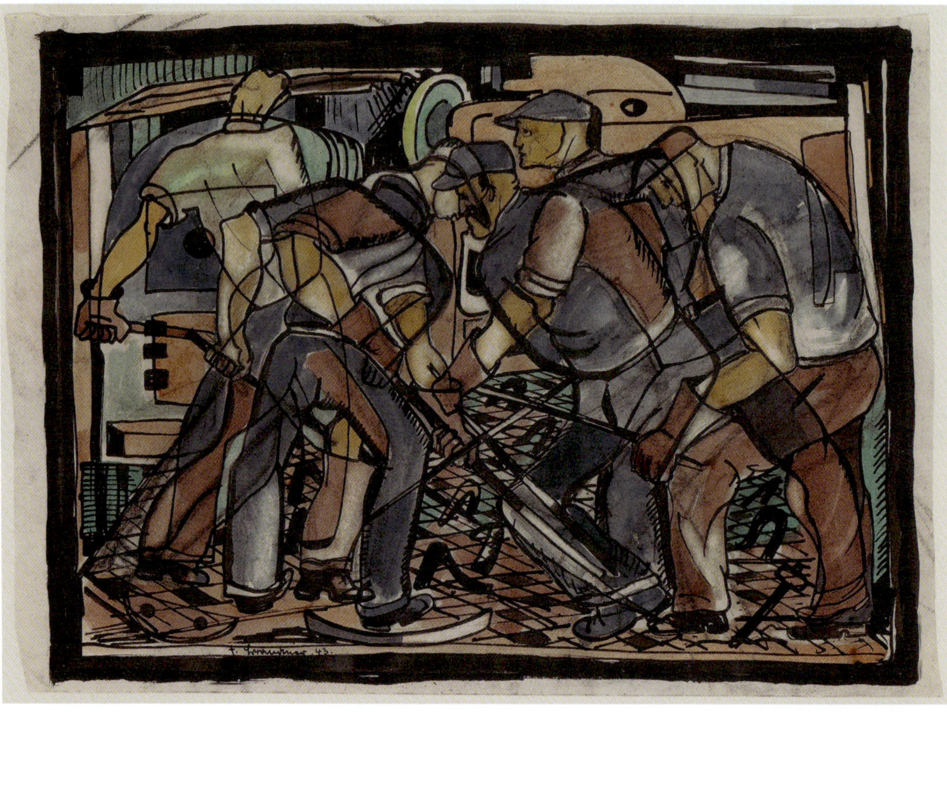

Fritz Brandtner

Born in Germany, Brandtner immigrated to Canada in 1928, settling first in Winnipeg and then moving in 1934 to Montreal, where he became part of both the modern art milieu and the city's progressive left-wing faction. A member of the Co-operative Commonwealth Federation (the CCF, forerunner of the New Democratic Party, the NDP) and deeply concerned with the social function of art, Brandtner devoted much of his time to art education among the disadvantaged, as well as being active in several national artists' organizations. In 1939, Brandtner was appointed first secretary of the Contemporary Arts Society, although he resigned a year later owing to differences of opinion about which little is known. He was also involved in the Federation of Canadian Artists, founded during the Kingston Conference of 1941.[36] He would serve as vice-president of the Canadian Society of Graphic Art from 1938 to 1940, of the Canadian Society of Painters in Water Colour from 1941 to 1943, and of the Canadian Group of Painters from 1944 to 1948.

The 1940s: The Multiple Faces of Abstraction

During the first half of the 1940s, Brandtner frequently exhibited works representing the war and wartime factory labourers. Walter Abell was among the critics whose attention was captured by the artist's images on these themes. In his review of the exhibition *Drawings of Canadian War Industries by Fritz Brandtner and Louis Muhlstock*, published in the October–November 1943 issue of *Canadian Art*, Abell compared the works by Muhlstock (1904–2001) – whose approach he considered too "immediate," unduly focused on the individual worker, isolated from his surroundings, too realistic and static, lacking in the "national effort" spirit – to Brandtner's, whose more abstract character he favoured. Abell was not crusading for some form of propaganda art, however: what interested him in Brandtner's works was above all the interior, Expressionist vision they conveyed, and their geometric, abstractionist design (ills. 24 and 25). Abell found Brandtner's approach convincing because its "semi-abstract" interpretation so fittingly reflected the abstract character of the industrial world:

ill. 24 (*opposite, top*)
Fritz Brandtner
Night Shift, 1943

ill. 25 – p. 72 (*opposite, bottom*)
Fritz Brandtner
Shaping Block, 1943

> But the key to Brandtner's success in the best examples is in the underlying and overlying structure of their semi-abstract design. Lines, colours, spaces, interplay dynamically with each other and become a visual embodiment of the forces and tensions, the piston thrusts and hammer blows, of modern industry. The industrial world in its essence is one of abstract forces and geometrical forms. Hence it lends itself perfectly to the prismatic vision in terms of which Brandtner sees it.[37]

Abell drew a parallel, then, between Brandtner's abstraction and the essential nature of industry, but he also saw it as expressing the intensity and febrility of the war effort.

Although Brandtner did not take part in Contemporary Arts Society exhibitions during the 1940s, he did show works in numerous other annual group exhibitions, including those organized by the Canadian Group of Painters. From time to time his contributions to the latter would earn a brief critical mention. In 1942, for example, Robert Ayre opened his review of the Canadian Group of Painters show by declaring that what struck him principally was the growing place being given to abstraction and semi-abstraction. He emphasized the dominance of Lawren Harris, and also noted the contributions of Webber and Borduas (*Harpe brune* [*Brown Harp*], 1941).[38] He even included Brandtner's 1941 painting *Four Nuns*[39] in the category of abstractions, since, despite the fact that the image represented human figures, all the emphasis was on its "dramatic design."[40]

On the occasion of the 1944 Canadian Group of Painters exhibition, a review in the *Gazette* laconically noted Brandtner's interest in war factory welders.[41] When the exhibition was shown in Winnipeg, Charles Nichols declared that he had become a little bored by the subject of welders, but that he was drawn to a Brandtner landscape also on view – although he did compare it to a "rag rug."[42] In the spring 1949 issue of *Canadian Art*, Robert Ayre expressed disappointment in that year's Canadian Group of Painters show, asserting that it was generally rather weak and suffered from a lack of representatives from francophone

ill. 28
Fritz Brandtner
City, 1948

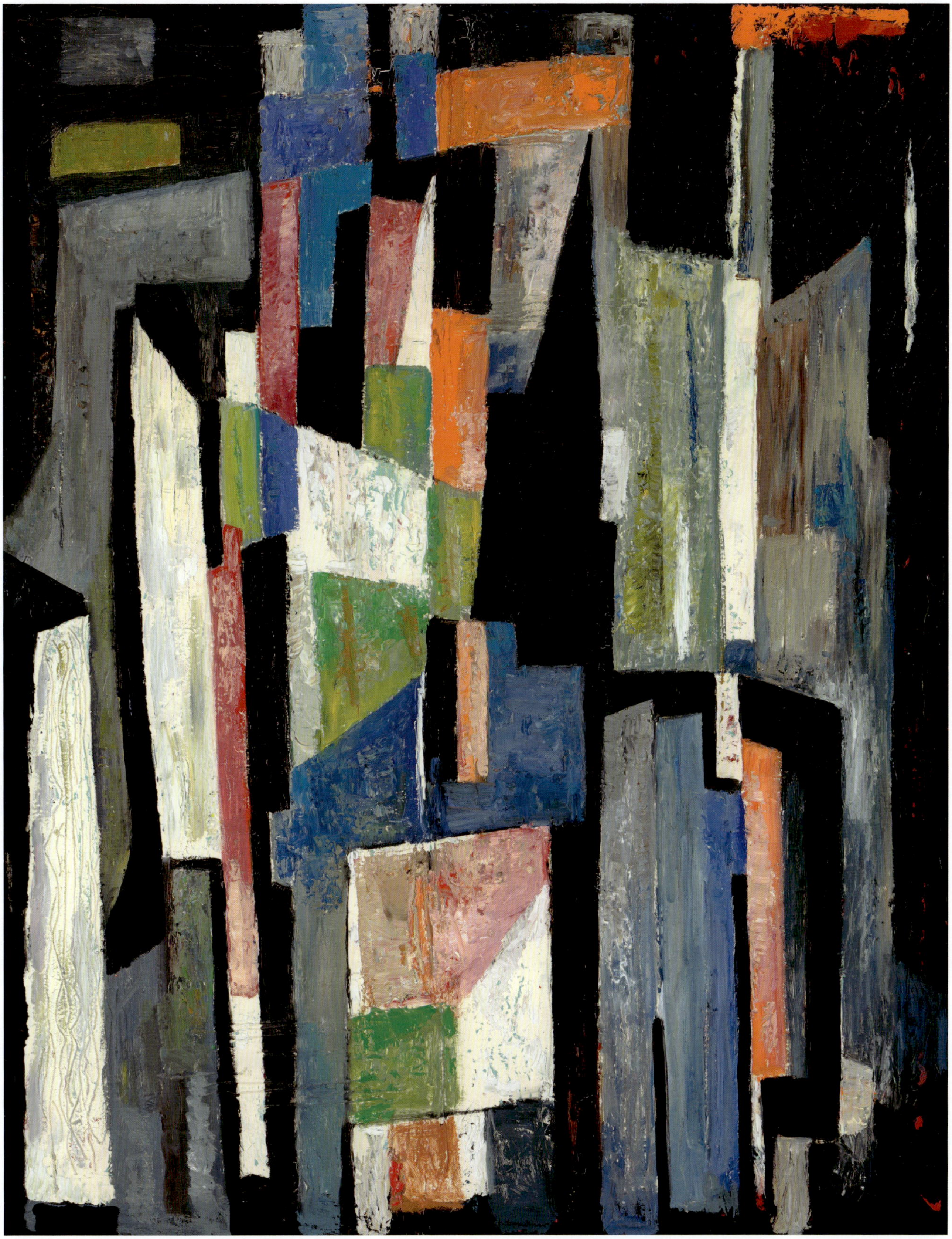

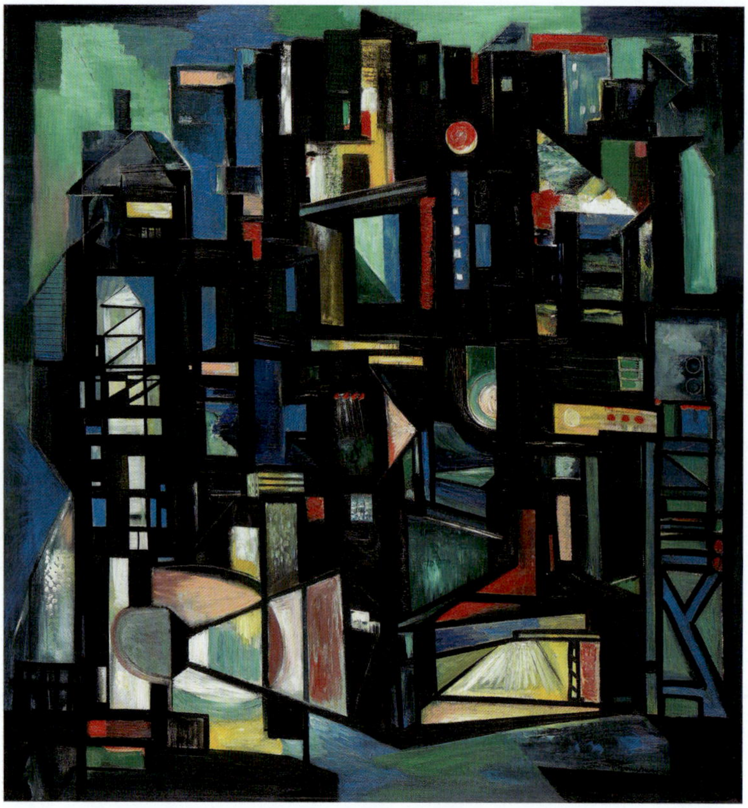

Quebec. Among the few works he did single out for mention was Brandtner's *City from a Night Train, No. 2*, which he described as "massive, intense, bursting with life, yet held within the bounds of a rigid scheme."[43]

I have selected a few of Brandtner's cityscapes from among his sizeable oeuvre, since this theme, by which he was so often inspired, effectively illustrates the diversity of styles he adopted. These include Expressionism, as in the astonishing *Bathing*, from 1937 (ill. 1), which depicts both nude bathers and a clothed female figure against the backdrop of a harbour scene. He also took a Cubist approach,

ill. 26
Fritz Brandtner
City from a Night Train, No. 2, about 1947

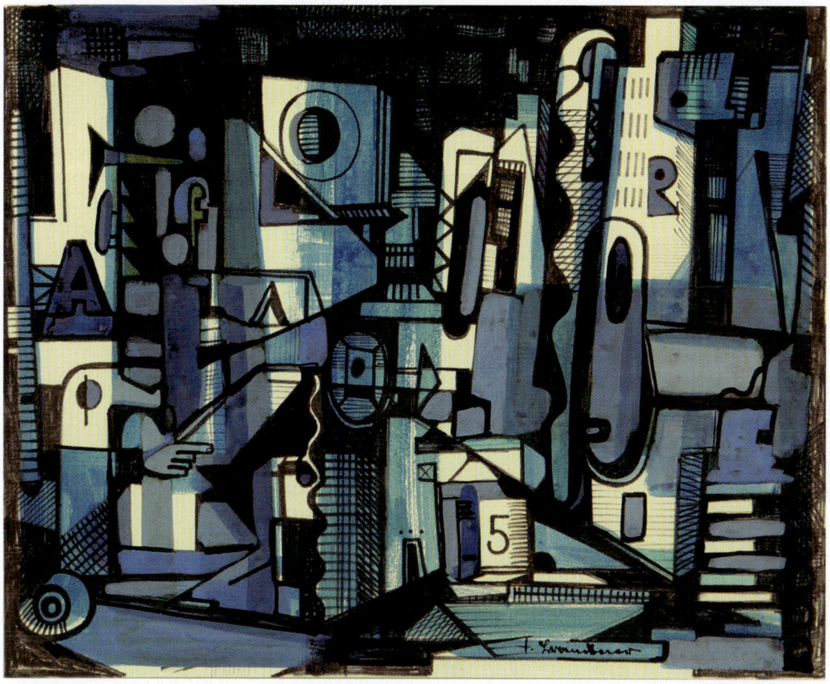

ill. 27
Fritz Brandtner
Untitled (City Abstract), about 1947

sometimes rather timidly, as in the 1938 painting *The Montreal Harbour* (ill. 2), where formal fragmentation is almost entirely limited to the shafts of light, or more assertively, as in *Untitled (City Abstract)* from about 1947. But he also came quite close to pure abstraction, as in the 1948 painting *City*, in which the black silhouette of a church steeple is the only clue to the context of the image's powerfully vertical geometric forms.

Clearly, although many of Brandtner's works from the 1940s were devoted to the subject of war, he also explored other themes and continued to experiment with a range of styles. Moreover, his practice encompassed various artistic modes, supports, and mediums, and he produced linocuts, screenprints, watercolours, and gouaches, which he exhibited at various events organized by associations of printmakers and watercolourists. One of his contributions to an exhibition held by the Canadian Society of Painters in Water Colour prompted a reviewer to reflect on the limits of the medium:

> A good example was Fritz Brandtner's Equestrian Study. This is a big stylized work of horses and riders, with plenty of strong orange and blue in it. Admittedly, the technique is mixed, that is to say it is not, in the most literal sense, *pure* water colour. But that is not the point.[44]

The critic, evidently not at all put out by the society's willingness to exhibit less traditional approaches to watercolour, declared how remarkable it was that developments within this rich medium were resulting in the execution of works whose power rivalled that of contemporary oil painting.

The work described in the review was likely related to *Men and Horses*, a screenprint that, with its vivid chromatic contrasts, the nudity of its horseback figures, and its non-descriptive palette of pure colours, is entirely in the German Expressionist tradition. This work in turn recalls the small didactic drawings that Brandtner had executed for an advertisement that appeared in the *Globe and Mail* on 27 January 1945, announcing the exhibition *Excursion in Abstract*, presented at Eaton's Fine Art Galleries in Toronto. It consists of a series of four images of a group of horses that moves progressively from realism to abstraction. No information has so far come to light concerning the precise content of this exhibition, which featured works by Fritz Brandtner, Henry Eveleigh, Lawren Harris, Edna Taçon, and Gordon Webber, nor about the one titled *Exhibition of Non-objective Paintings by Fritz Brandtner, Henry Eveleigh and Gordon Webber*, which had been presented a couple of months earlier in Montreal, from 8 to 26 November 1944, in the Art Association's lecture hall.[45] Reviews of this show by Montreal critics offer a glimpse of what it contained, but unfortunately their descriptions are not always clear. It is possible to identify several works by Gordon Webber and Henry Eveleigh from their articles, but references to Brandtner are less informative. For example, although François

Gagnon (pseudonym of François Rinfret) of *La Presse* stated that the artists resolutely avoided "any representation of reality," he gave few details about the works, which – since they employed a variety of mediums (collage, photographs, wood) – he described as "making use of methods foreign to painting." Speaking of Brandtner, Gagnon revealed only that he divided the canvas with "small pieces of wood."[46] An anonymous reviewer writing for the *Gazette* advised readers to keep an open mind when looking at the works, which he or she praised effusively, while nevertheless remarking that their design sometimes resembled what one might doodle while on the phone or when bored at a concert. Although each artist's approach was described, all that was said of Brandtner was that he displayed "a generally firmer structure in his imaginings and has evolved some nice colour arrangements."[47] The most enthusiastic review is signed D.S. (undoubtedly Dorothy Sangster). Writing in the *Standard*, she acknowledged that the exhibition had been the source of considerable controversy, but nevertheless maintained that it was interesting for three reasons: first, each artist's approach was entirely individual; second, although all the works were characterized by brilliant colours and a total freedom of expression, they remained entirely distinct; and finally, each artist expressed their own "necessity," using their own personal methods. As we shall see later, her descriptions of Webber and Eveleigh's works were more detailed and discerning than those of her colleagues, but Brandtner seems to have left her somewhat perplexed. "Brandtner shows considerable skill with colour," she wrote, "but leaves the impression that he is doodling with coloured squares, circles and triangles."[48]

Taken together, the critics' accounts of Brandtner's contributions to this exhibition tell us little. All that can be deduced is that they included abstractions featuring geometric forms and bright colours. *Abstract Composition*, *Design No. 6*,[49] and *Construction* are examples of this type of non-objective, constructive, dynamic, highly coloured abstraction, which Brandtner practised at the same time as a more Expressionist style that still retained some figurative elements.

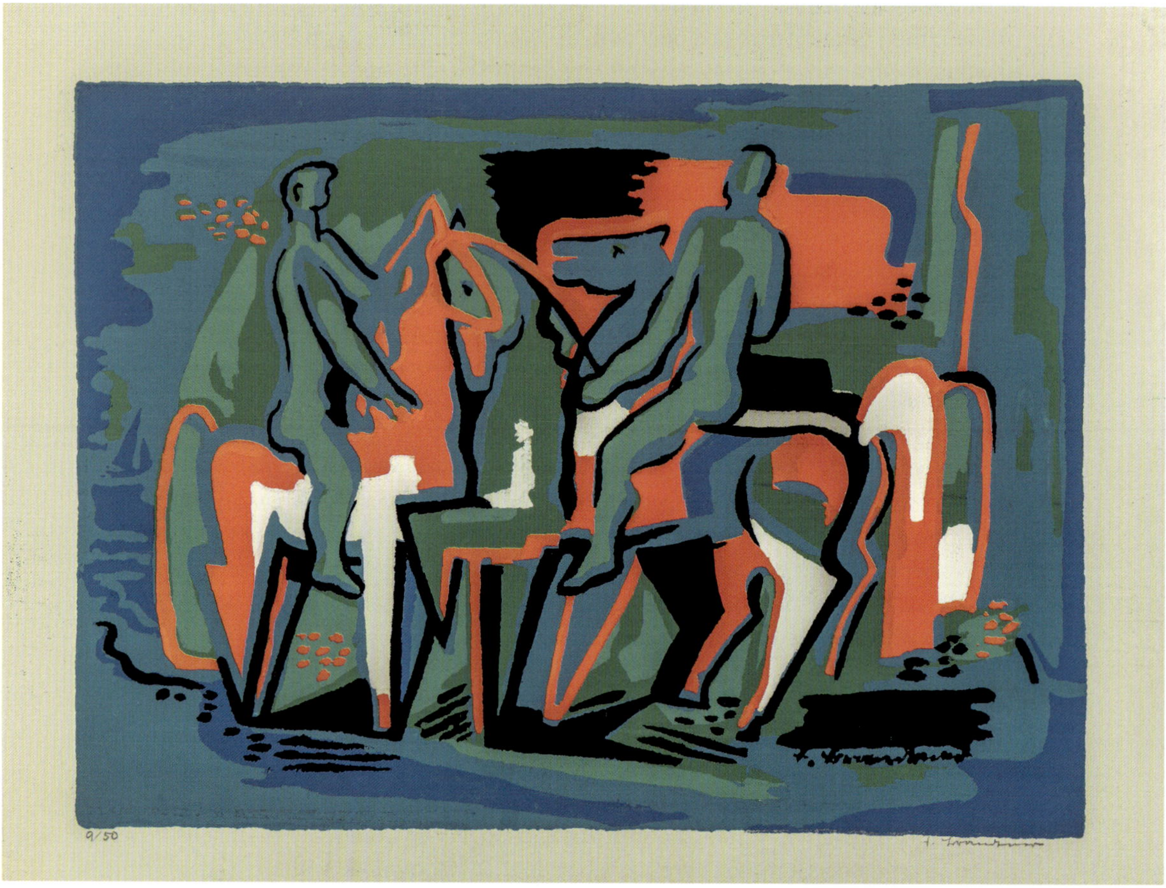

ill. 29
Fritz Brandtner
Men and Horses, about 1945–50

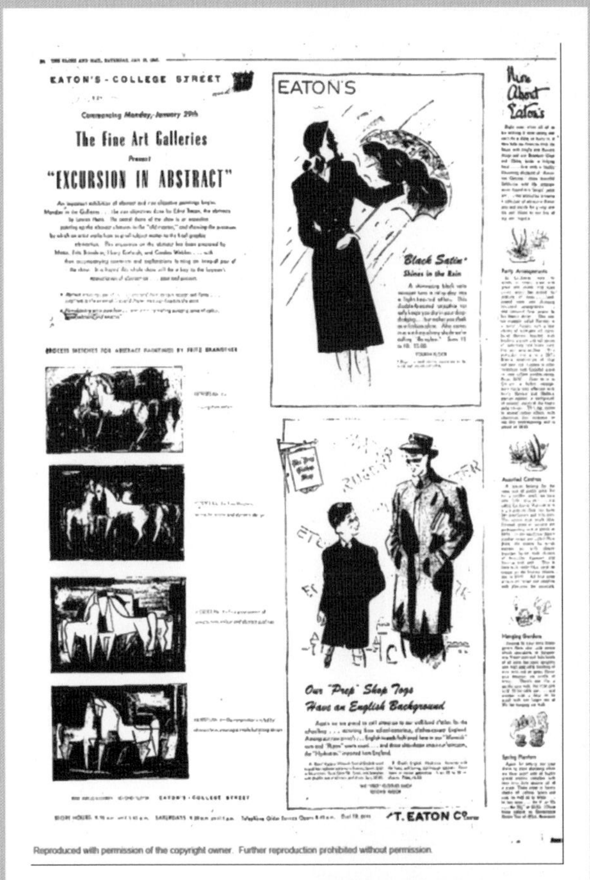
EATON'S - COLLEGE STREET

Commencing Monday, January 29th

The Fine Art Galleries

Present

"EXCURSION IN ABSTRACT"

PROCESS SKETCHES FOR ABSTRACT PAINTINGS BY FRITZ BRANDTNER

EATON'S COLLEGE STREET

Commencing Monday, January 29th

The Fine Art Galleries
present

"EXCURSION IN ABSTRACT"

An important exhibition of abstract and non-objective paintings begins Monday in the Galleries ... the non-objectives done by Edna Taçon, the abstracts by Lawren Harris. The central theme of the show is an exposition pointing up the abstract elements in the "old masters," showing the processes by which an artist works from original subject matter to the final graphic abstraction. This exhibition on the abstract has been prepared by Messrs. Fritz Brandtner, Henry Eveleigh, and Gordon Webber ... with their accompanying comments and explanations forming an integral part of the show. It is hoped this whole show will be a key to the layman's appreciation of abstract art past and present.

* Abstract paintings are those that proceed from certain recognizable forms ... simplified to the essential lines and shapes most significant to the artist.

* Non-objective art is pure form ... proposing nothing except a sense of colour, space relations and emotion.

Process sketches for abstract paintings by Fritz Brandtner

Horses No. 1 – Drawing from nature

Horses No. 2 – Simplification, search for action and dynamic design

Horses No. 3 – First arrangement of composition, colour and abstract qualities

Horses No. 4 – The composition is ruled by abstract form, creating a simple but strong design

ill. 30
Screenshot of an Eaton's advertisement describing the exhibition *Excursion in Abstract*, featuring works by Fritz Brandtner, Henry Eveleigh, Lawren Harris, Edna Taçon, and Gordon Webber, presented at Eaton's Fine Art Galleries in Toronto, *Globe and Mail* (Toronto), 27 January 1945, 34

Despite all efforts, it has proved impossible to find a high-quality image of this advertisement. The text has been transcribed to facilitate reading.

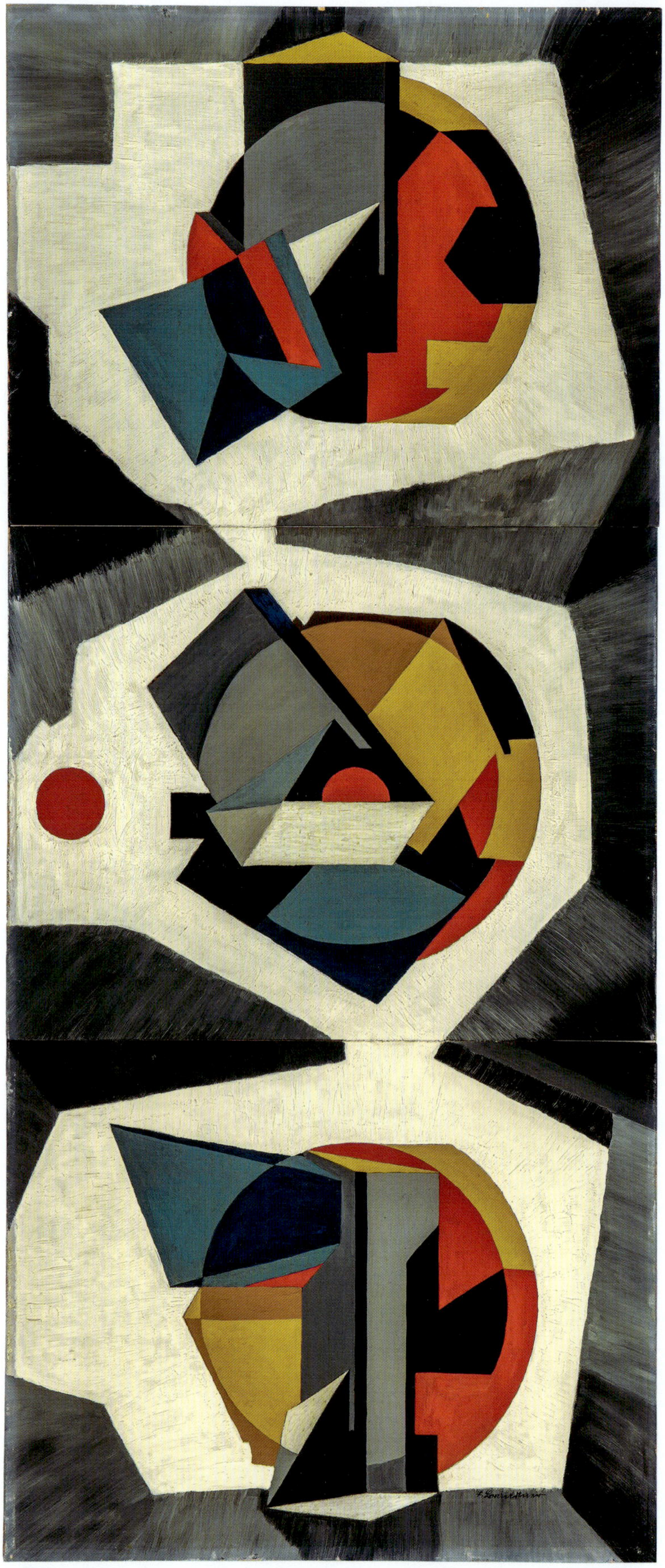

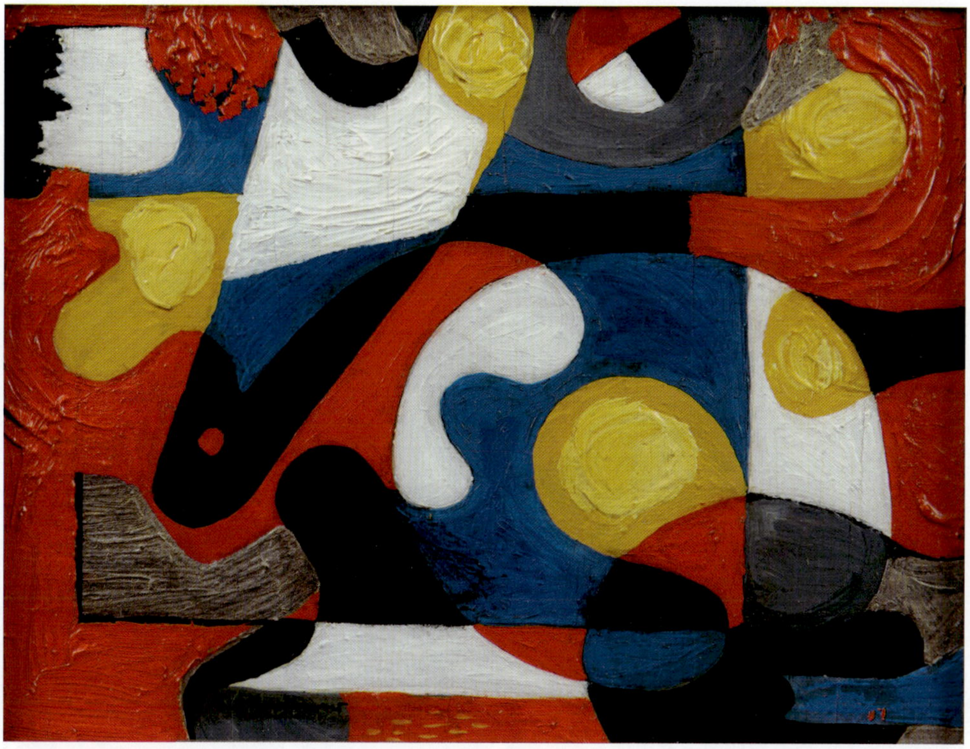

By the end of the 1940s, Brandtner was one of the painters invariably mentioned by critics when listing Montreal's contemporary artists – outside the francophone milieu, needless to say. And, as we have seen, Brandtner would be (along with Henry Eveleigh) one of the two participants representing "non-figurative art" at the conference organized by the Federation of Canadian Artists in 1949 and held at the Art Association of Montreal.

ill. 31 (*opposite*)
Fritz Brandtner
Abstract Composition, 1940

ill. 32 (*above*)
Fritz Brandtner
Design No. 6, n.d.

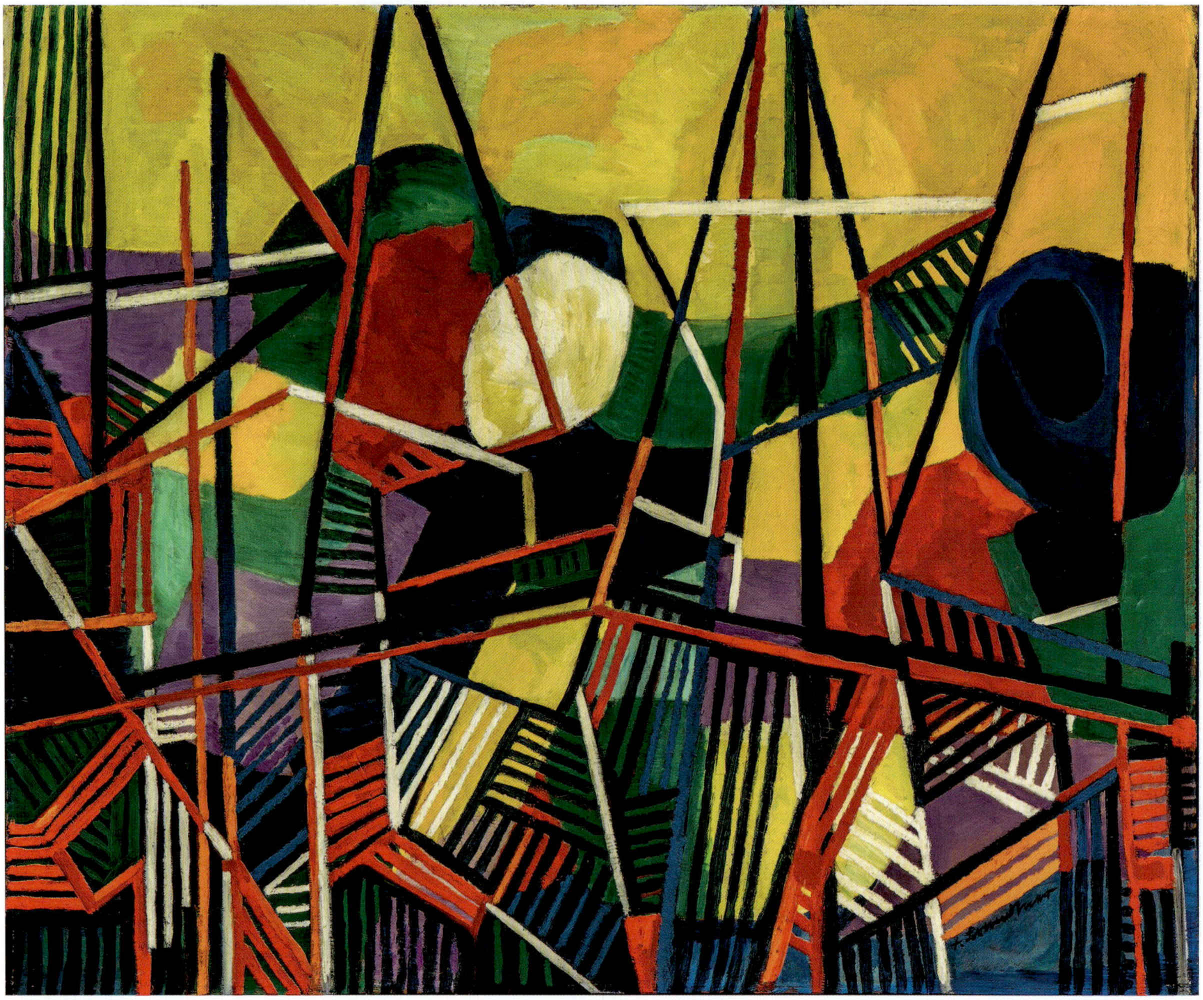

ill. 33
Fritz Brandtner
Construction, about 1938

The 1950s: Art as Experience

Brandtner's approach did not alter significantly during the 1950s, and he continued to employ different styles – Expressionist, Cubist, abstract – to express his vision of art as experience. To complete the selection of this artist's works I have chosen two landscapes, a genre he practised throughout his life. In some examples, such as *Road to Gaspé*, Brandtner divides the pictorial space into a network of expressive lines that frame and overlay areas of vivid colour. In others, like *St. Lawrence at Night, Matane*, he opts for more geometric forms that increase the impression of abstraction, while nonetheless remaining highly expressive.

The Musée d'art de Joliette owns a series of eight drawings, collectively titled *Cosmos*, which, though undated, were certainly executed during the late 1950s or early 1960s. In each case, the entire surface is covered by a dynamically complex linear network, within which are embedded a variety of motifs, including planets, atom-like structures, and other circular, ocular, or amoeba-shaped forms. Various types of aircraft also traverse these cosmic worlds, which simultaneously evoke scientific progress and the conquest of space that fascinated so many in the postwar period.

A diary that Brandtner kept from the late 1950s to the start of 1960 offers a few clues concerning what some might see as the eclecticism of his practice. Jean-Pierre Labiau, author of the catalogue on Brandtner's work published by the Montreal Museum of Fine Arts in 2003, has studied the thoughts recorded in this diary and revealed that, for Brandtner, art was a formal exploration that could follow a variety of paths in its quest to "discover the essence of things, reduce them to a symbol of a line or a shape, then re-create them into pattern (symbols), units of pattern that will form the picture, a work of art."[50] But that was not all: art also possessed what could be seen as a pedagogical function. For Brandtner, Labiau explains, "the art of the pedagogue is to awaken new creative forces, while Expressionism serves to awaken the senses, Cubism the intellect, and kineticism acuteness of vision."[51] It is a conception of artistic creation completely devoid of stylistic dogmatism. In Brandtner's view, diversity – of techniques, subjects, objects, materials – offered a way for an artist to be of his time:

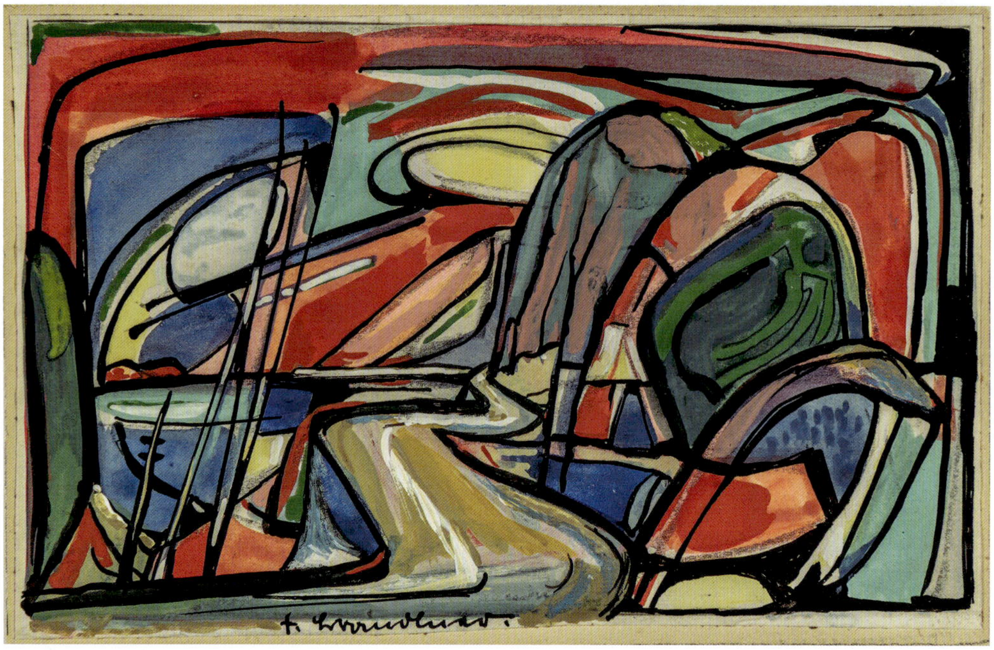

As free men we can no more imitate the styles and lives and thoughts of other times and other men. We must continue to develop new form, new space concepts equal to the new ideas of life we have to set stirring in the world. The new world has produced new machines and new materials. Let us also invent new form, new space concepts for our new ways of life. Let us liberate our vision. Let us have faith in our own individuality.[52]

ill. 34
Fritz Brandtner
Road to Gaspé, n.d.

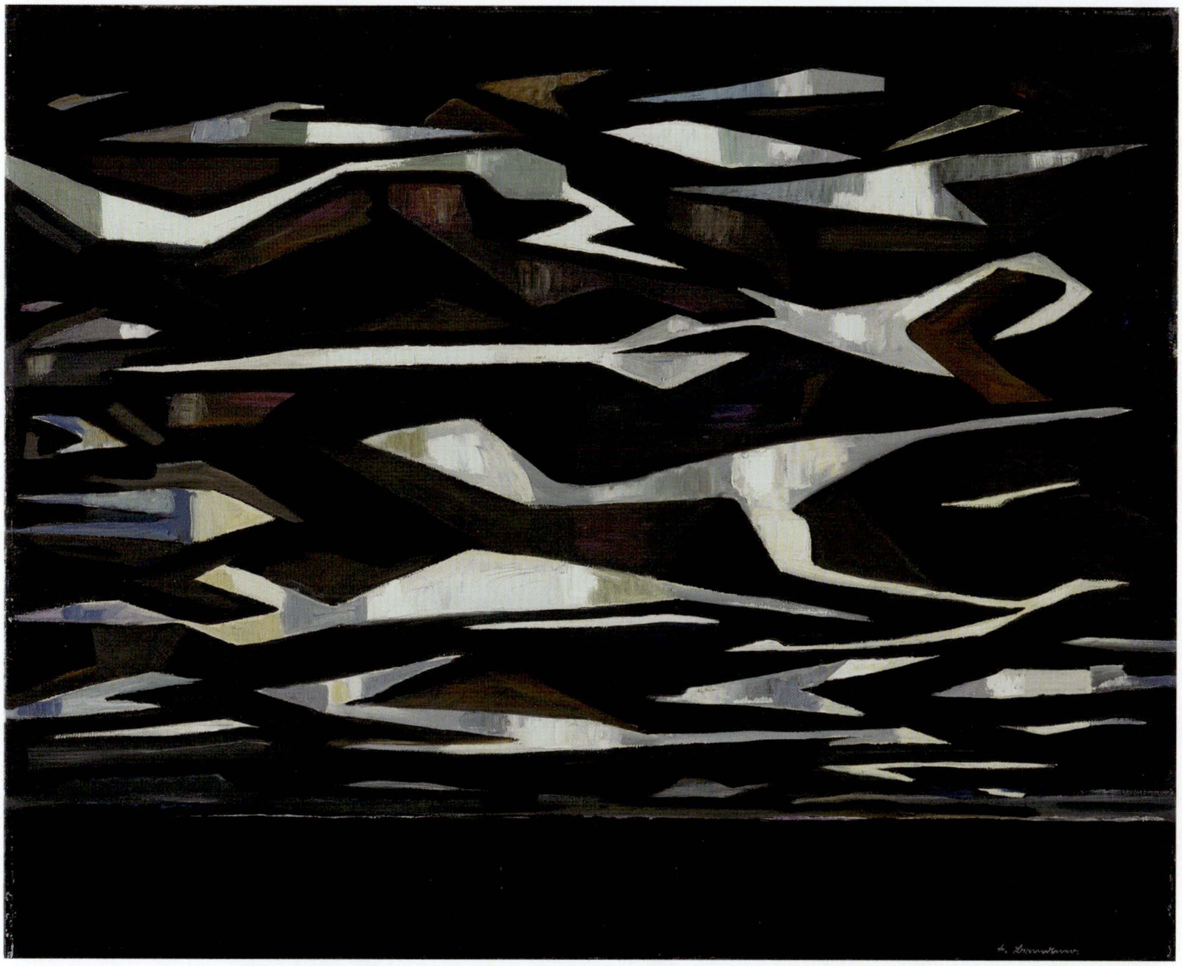

ill. 35
Fritz Brandtner
St. Lawrence at Night, Matane, about 1959

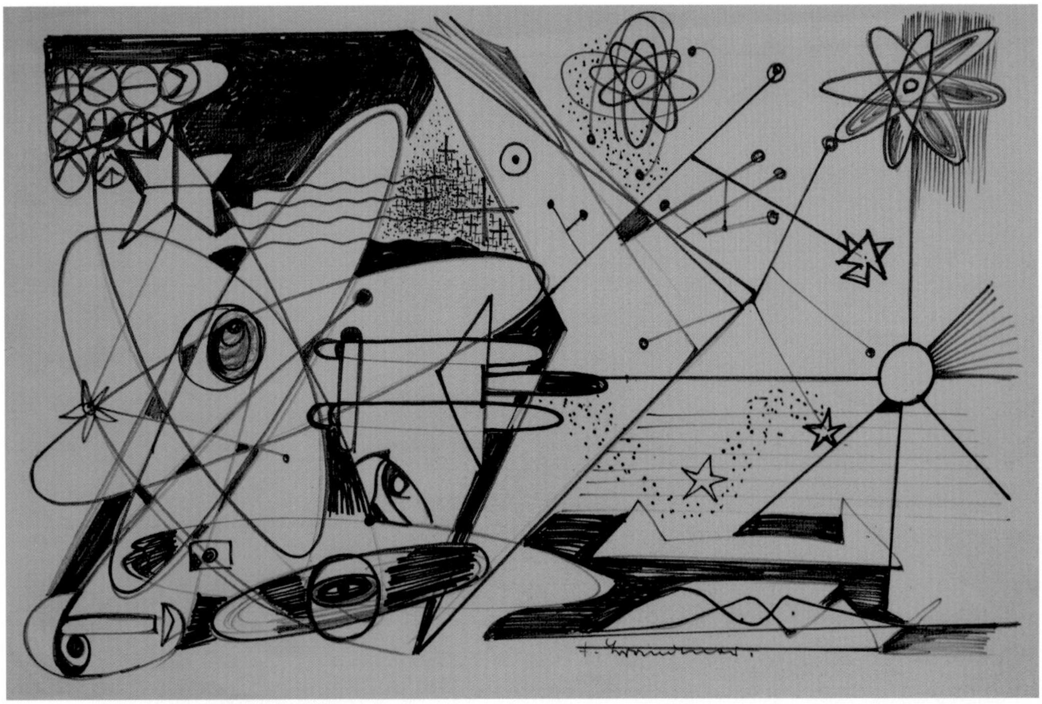

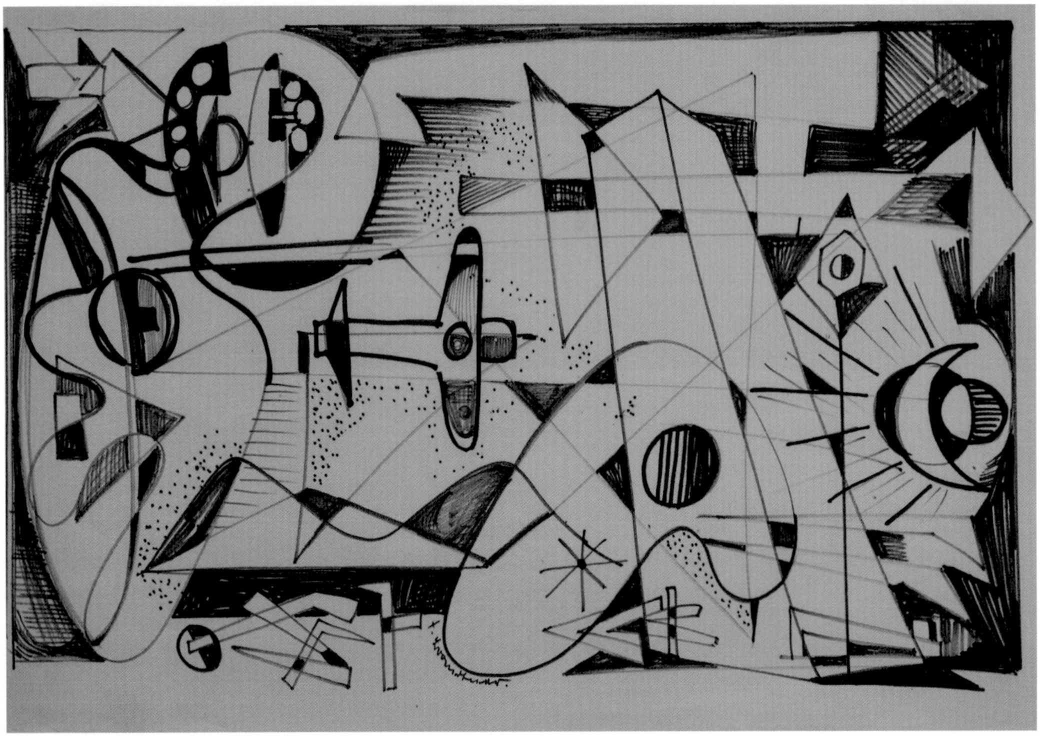

ill. 36 (*top*)
Fritz Brandtner
Cosmos VII, between 1958 and 1962

ill. 37 (*bottom*)
Fritz Brandtner
Cosmos I, between 1958 and 1962

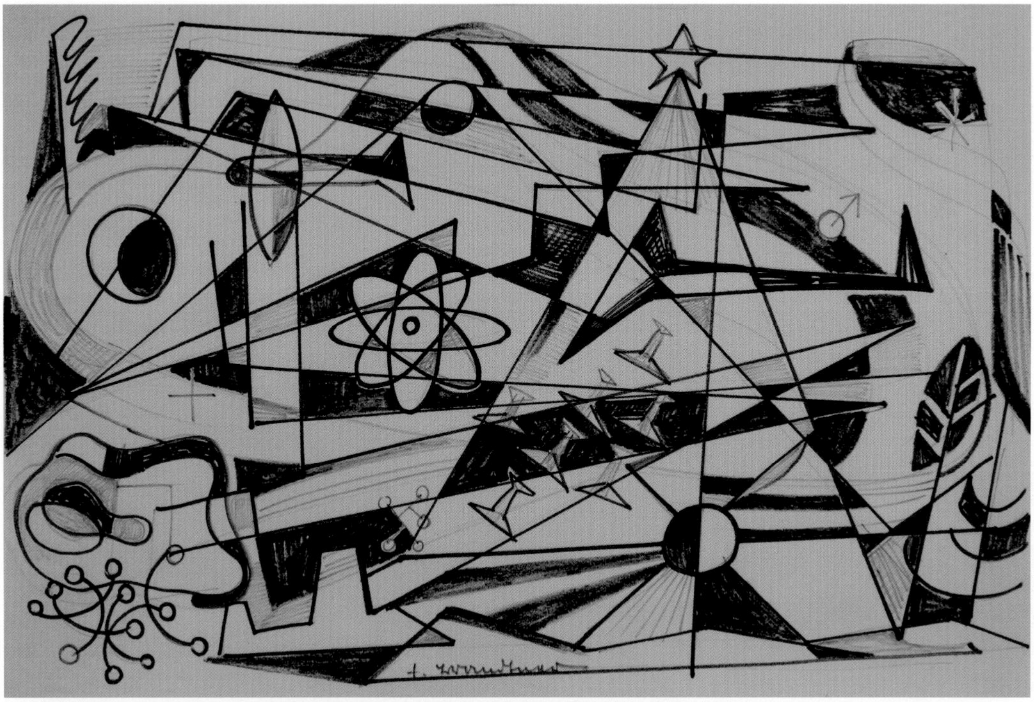

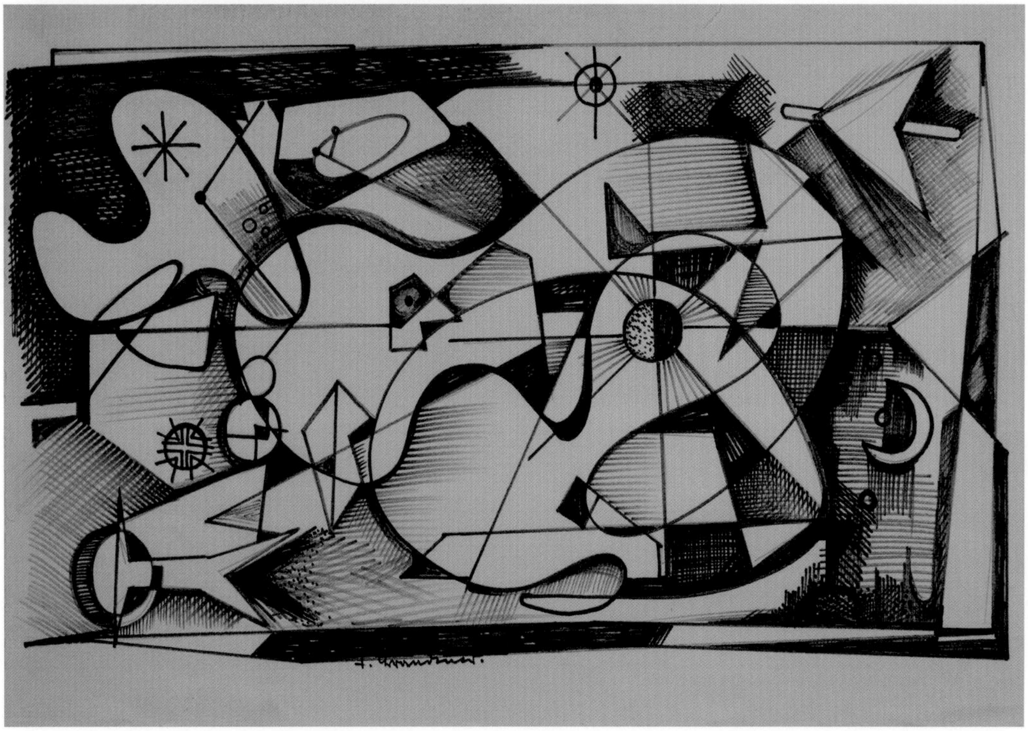

ill. 38 (*top*)
Fritz Brandtner
Cosmos III, between 1958 and 1962

ill. 39 (*bottom*)
Fritz Brandtner
Cosmos VI, between 1958 and 1962

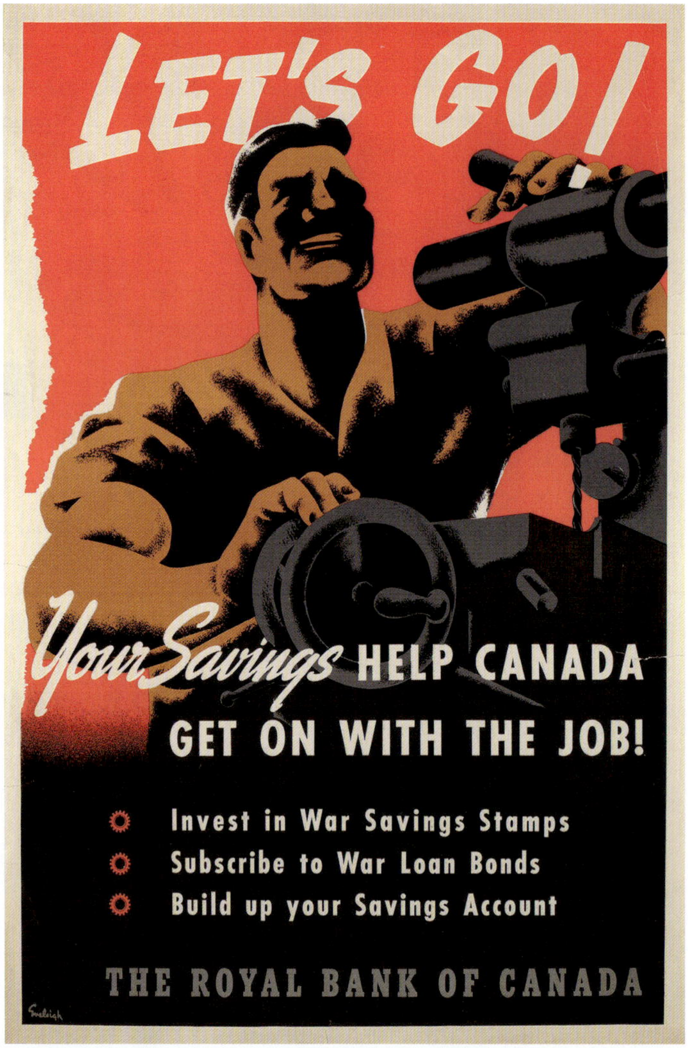

ill. 40
Henry Eveleigh
Let's Go! Your Savings Help Canada Get On with the Job!, about 1941–45
Fundraising poster

Henry Eveleigh

Henry Eveleigh, who was born in Shanghai, received his art education at the Slade School of Fine Art in London, where he graduated in 1934. After travels in Europe and a return to Shanghai, he immigrated to Canada in 1938. Following a short stay in Vancouver he moved to Montreal, where he joined the group of artists who would shortly be founding the Contemporary Arts Society but also began developing ties in the graphic design milieu. At the society's first exhibition, held at the Frank Stevens Gallery in 1939, he showed *Beach and Escape*, a painting that reflected the dual influence of Cubism and Surrealism – "of Freud and of Picasso," to paraphrase Reynald, critic for *La Presse*.[53] This indicates that Eveleigh's approach had changed considerably since his time at the Slade: two works in the collection of the University College London Art Museum, *Male Figure Seated in a Chair* (a nude that earned him a first prize for painting in 1934) and *Recreation: The Interior of an Inn with Figures*, also from 1934, both reflect the social realism common during the interwar period.[54]

When Henry Eveleigh arrived in Montreal, its art scene was on the brink of radical change. Throughout the 1940s, like his colleague Fritz Brandtner, Eveleigh would exhibit the results of a practice that encompassed both non-objective abstractions and works that retained references to the real world but employed a vocabulary derived from Cubism or Surrealism. Some of the latter explored themes related to the war, although far less overtly than the propaganda posters he was commissioned to execute – in his parallel role as a professional graphic designer – by the Department of National War Services.[55]

Between 22 November and 15 December 1940, the Contemporary Arts Society held an exhibition at the Art Association of Montreal called *Art of Our Day in Canada*, which brought together some fifty artists, including a number of non-members. One of the most thoughtful reviews was published in the *Standard* by Robert Ayre, in which he speculated on the "art of today" in relation to the history of modern art in Canada, but particularly in the context of grave anxiety caused by the war.

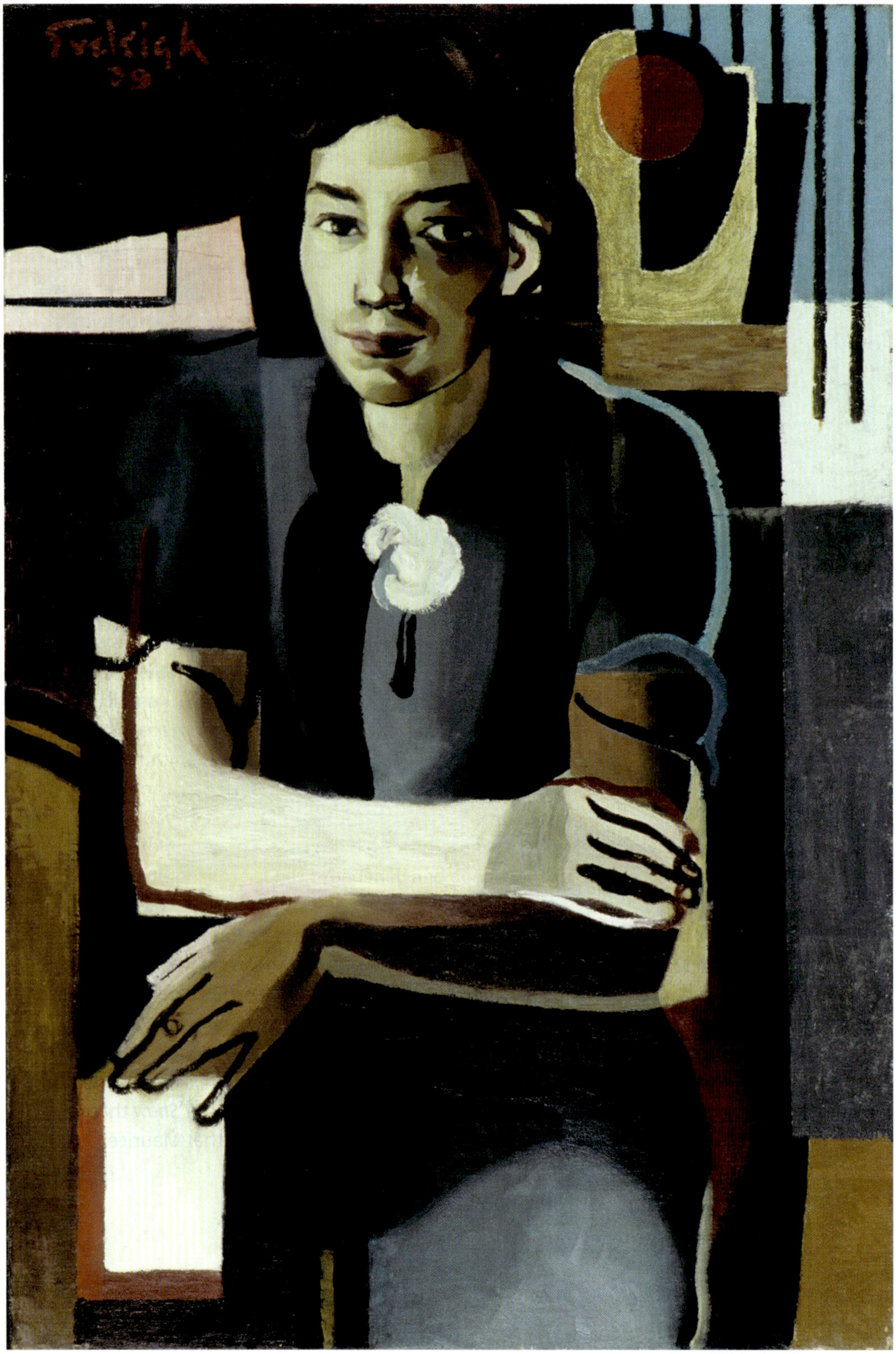

The 1942 Exhibition: Cubism, Surrealism, and Abstraction

The exhibition *Paintings by Louis Muhlstock and Henry Eveleigh*, held at the Art Association of Montreal in November 1942, represented a key moment in the artist's career, since it drew considerable critical attention. Eveleigh's work was enthusiastically received by such francophone critics as Pierre Daniel (pseudonym of Robert Élie), Henri Girard, Maurice Huot,[59] Charles Doyon, and Jean-Charles Harvey. However, Dorothy Sangster was the only anglophone reviewer to comment on his work in any detail, while the critics for the *Montreal Daily Star* and the *Gazette* limited themselves to brief, rather hostile comments.[60]

The practices of Louis Muhlstock and Henry Eveleigh displayed major stylistic differences, and the critics consequently analyzed their works quite separately. In fact, the "duo" exhibitions organized by the museum were not necessarily designed to form a coherent whole. At the time, artists could submit a solo exhibition proposal to the Art Association of Montreal, which, for a variety of reasons, might decide to unite two or three artists in the same space under a collective title. That this was the case here is indicated by a letter dated 17 July 1942 that Muhlstock addressed to Dr Charles F. Martin, then director of the Art Association of Montreal, proposing a one-man exhibition of his work.[61] Muhlstock subsequently found himself exhibiting alongside Eveleigh, an artist who, though a fellow member of the Contemporary Arts Society, had adopted a very different approach.

Nothing is known today of most of the twenty-four works exhibited by Eveleigh in this exhibition.[62] The exceptions are *The Fortune Teller*, *Mother and Child* – which is known from a study – one of two *Odalisques*, and possibly the painting titled *Emotion*, which I shall discuss later. Descriptions offered by the critics, however, together with the works reproduced in this catalogue, provide a relatively clear picture of what the exhibition must have contained. It is evident, first of all, that quite a few of the works were portraits, among them the aforementioned *Kit Shaw*, along with *The Fortune Teller*, which would be acquired by the Art Association of Montreal that same year and illustrated in the *Standard* on 21 November 1942. The known portraits and nudes show the clear influence of Cubism, as does the gouache *Mother and Child.* However, the study's

ill. 42
Henry Eveleigh
The Fortune Teller, 1939

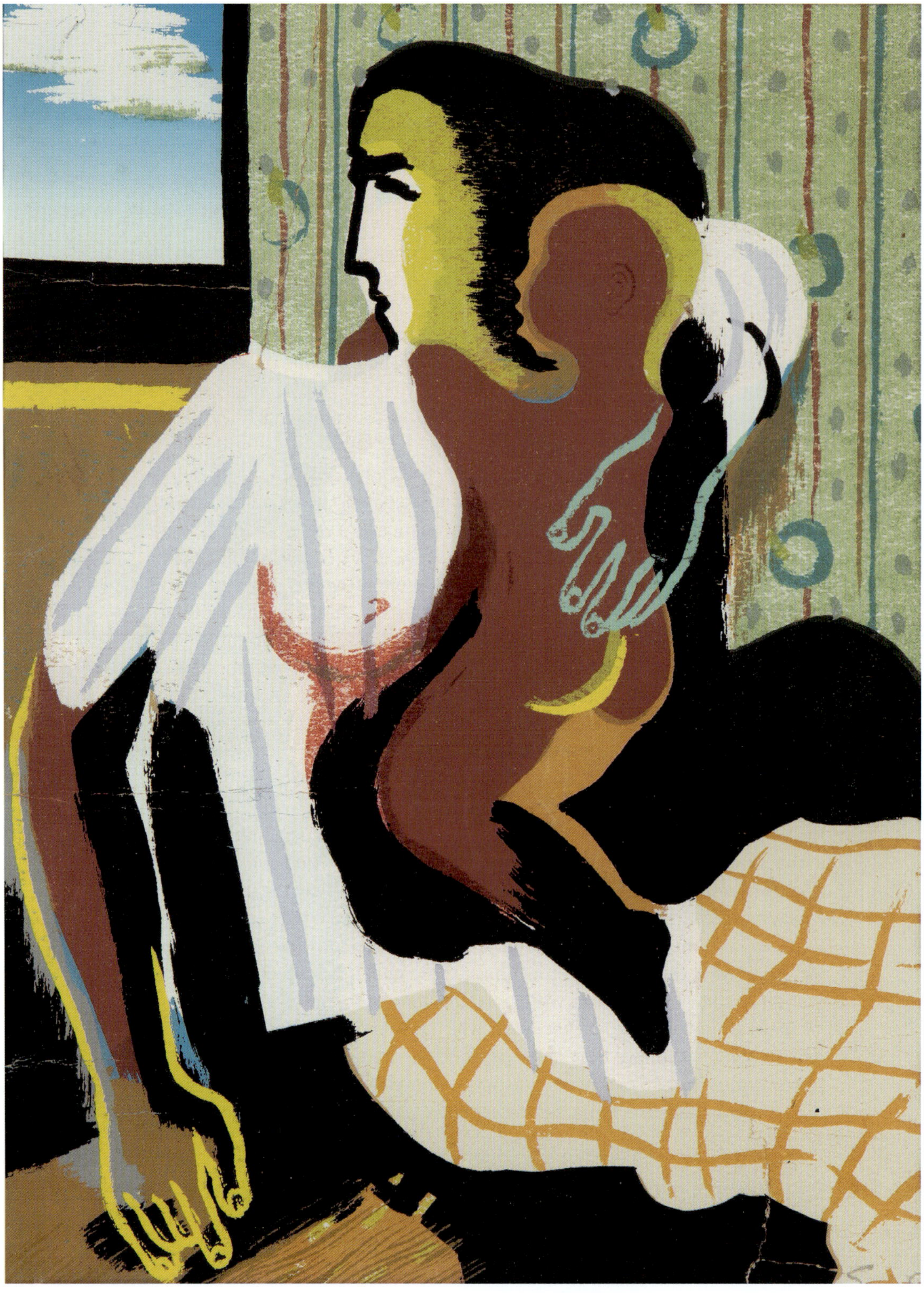

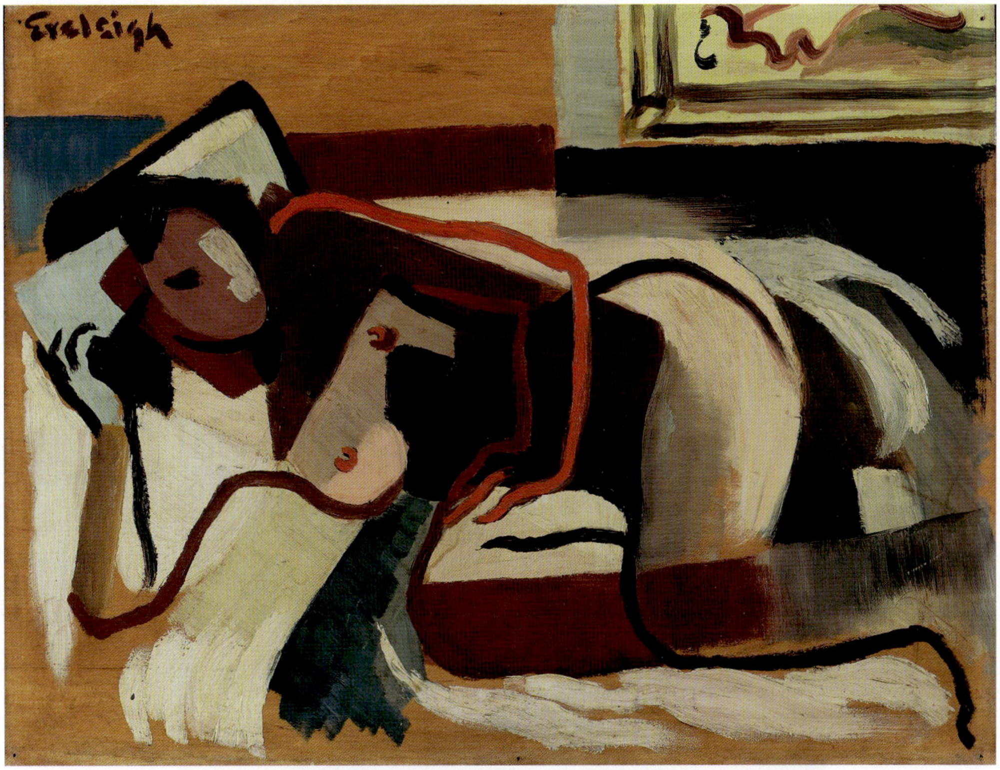

decorative areas of colour carry echoes of Matisse, and the arresting view of the sky through the window speaks more of Magritte than of the Quattrocento. These works are striking for the broad outlines that define the figures of the models, but the *Odalisque*'s body is overlaid by geometric forms that have no anatomical significance. The nudes appealed particularly to Dorothy Sangster, who reproduced one of them in her article. The highly positive comment beneath the image was accompanied by an acknowledgment, quite unusual for the time, of the negative consequences of reproduction: "Vivid colour, perfect in design and entirely sophisticated in effect, this picture unfortunately loses much by photographic reproduction." Emphasizing the formal qualities of Eveleigh's works, Sangster's article also includes this severe observation: "Artists and lovers of modern art will find Eveleigh's exhibition interesting and provocative; the average man, alas, intolerant of departure from accepted form, will probably dismiss it as 'queer.'"[63]

ill. 43 (*opposite*)
Henry Eveleigh
Study for Mother and Child, n.d.

ill. 44 (*above*)
Henry Eveleigh
Odalisque, 1938

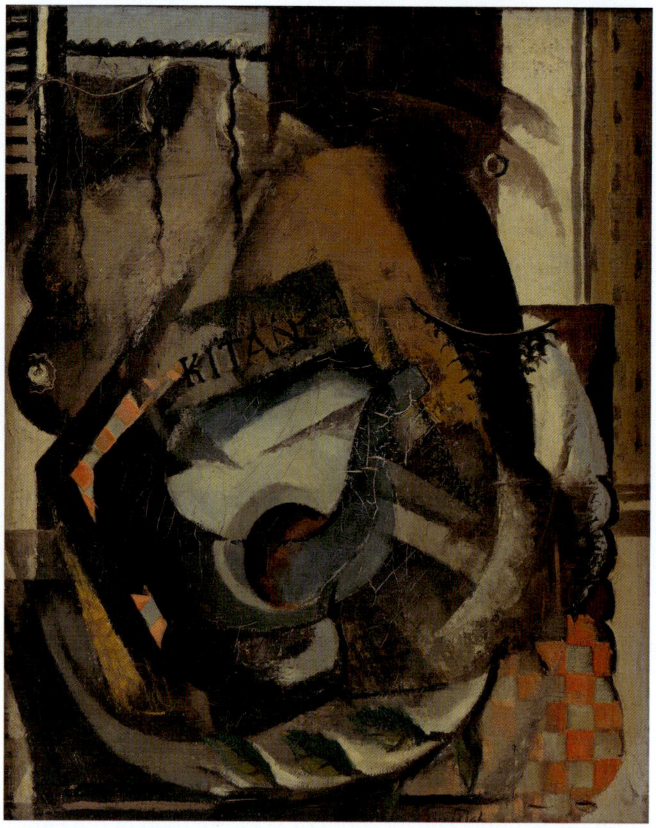

Also worth citing is Charles Doyon's charming description of one of the *Odalisques*:

> First of all there is this little *Odalisque*, with its delightfully intertwined limbs. In a pose much favoured by Matisse, plump flesh is encircled by a firm line that frames pale forms where, in less defined areas, a mysterious shadow blissfully lingers. This Odalisque, which adorns the invitation, is an enticing lure.[64]

The list of works also mentions a still life. If it resembled the one discovered in the artist's estate (ill. 45), the influence of Cubism was likely even more marked than in the nudes and portraits.

ill. 45
Henry Eveleigh
Still Life, n.d.

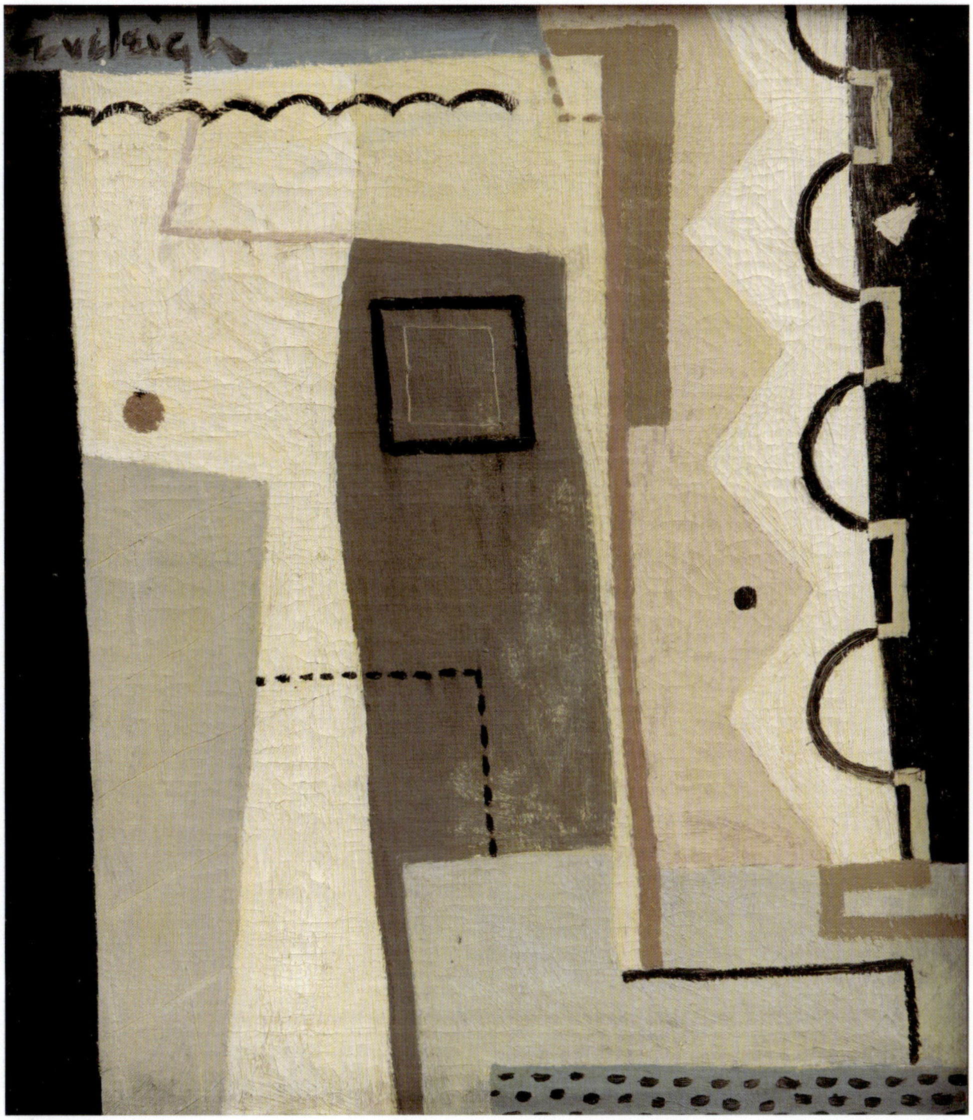

ill. 46
Henry Eveleigh
Stage Door, 1936

Eveleigh included in the show a few paintings with titles like *Abstraction Variation* and *Abstraction Project* that consisted of relatively geometric and dynamic abstract constructions. Among the critics who responded positively to these works was Pierre Daniel, who preferred them to the artist's "reveries à la Salvador Dali," which he judged less "successful" and rather "heavy," despite their "solid and ingenious" compositions. It would be in the abstractions, Daniel wrote, that composition "becomes more subtle and colour attains its greatest purity. The tones are very beautiful and Eveleigh displays a fine sense of harmony."[65] The critic even chose one of these paintings to illustrate his article – a work very similar to the one reproduced here (ill. 46).[66]

As for what Daniel describes as the "reveries à la Salvador Dali," they belong to another category of works that the critics had little difficulty in associating with Surrealism. Daniel mentions them in the brief survey that opens his review:

> The group of works Eveleigh presents is surprising first in its diversity. Sometimes, he composes his painting by starting with the model's actual forms, which he reveals with an abrupt and assured line; elsewhere, the forms unfurl freely in space, no longer evoking anything of the external world; or Eveleigh will give free rein to his dream and allow the image to float in the unreal, seizing it once again at the instant the dream has captured all the mysterious powers hidden in the depths of being.

While Pierre Daniel preferred the artist's pure abstractions to his Surrealist works, Henri Girard was evidently fascinated by the latter. He began his article, published in *Le Canada* on 20 November 1942, with the following words: "At the Art Gallery, Mr. Henry Eveleigh is presenting us with his version of Surrealism." His lengthy and rather poetic text includes a few descriptions that offer further glimpses of the paintings:

> *Elements*. A leafless tree next to a woman's shoe supports a wristwatch near a lake surrounded by hills: love, death, time, nature. In the same spirit, still in search of symbols, take another look at Eveleigh's exhibition.

Girard felt that spectators would undoubtedly appreciate the formal elements of the works, but would also be intrigued by their symbolism.

> Any man of taste (not necessarily someone who has benefited from a "classical" education), if he has trained his eye to appreciate interplays of line and colour, will instinctively like Eveleigh. He will enjoy solving the puzzles presented by certain canvases. But first he will see admirable symphonies of lines, forms and colours. Only after will he attempt to perceive the symbols that the artist employs to make the content of the subconscious visible.[67]

In his review, Charles Doyon also mentions a couple of the Surrealist works: *Week-End in Fall* – "an inhuman beach marked by clogs, bordered by trees and a mountain split from its own shadow" – and *Impedimenta* – "That arm, that insistent hand is of an all too obvious intent, and yet there is here suggestion of an irrevocable sign."[68]

Doyon situated Eveleigh's aesthetic approach "somewhere between Pellan's ideas and the theories of Borduas." He considered Borduas's interpretation of Surrealism more successful than Eveleigh's, however. The latter, he felt, imitated "some of the features seen often in Dali's work: incongruous objects, vivisection, fantasies. These traits denote a morbid type of Surrealism." He returned to the subject a little later: "*The Beach* and *Elements* can be associated with the kind of exaggerated Surrealism that Dali made fashionable. I remain unmoved by these lure-objects, these prompt-ornaments that, through trompe-l'œil or brilliance, spoil the painting." Like Pierre Daniel, Doyon preferred Eveleigh's abstractions, especially *Variation*, an "assemblage of colours related to the Cubism I have identified with Pellan." For Maurice Gagnon, Borduas, and several others, it will be recalled, abstraction (non-Automatiste abstraction) was the logical outcome of Cubism.[69]

From the critics' descriptions, we learn that, alongside the portraits and nudes inspired by Cubism, and a few "pure" abstractions, Eveleigh showed at least four compositions whose figurative motifs had been assembled by means of collage or juxtaposition. These visual "puzzles," arising apparently from the subconscious, offered further evidence of the artist's connection to Surrealism.

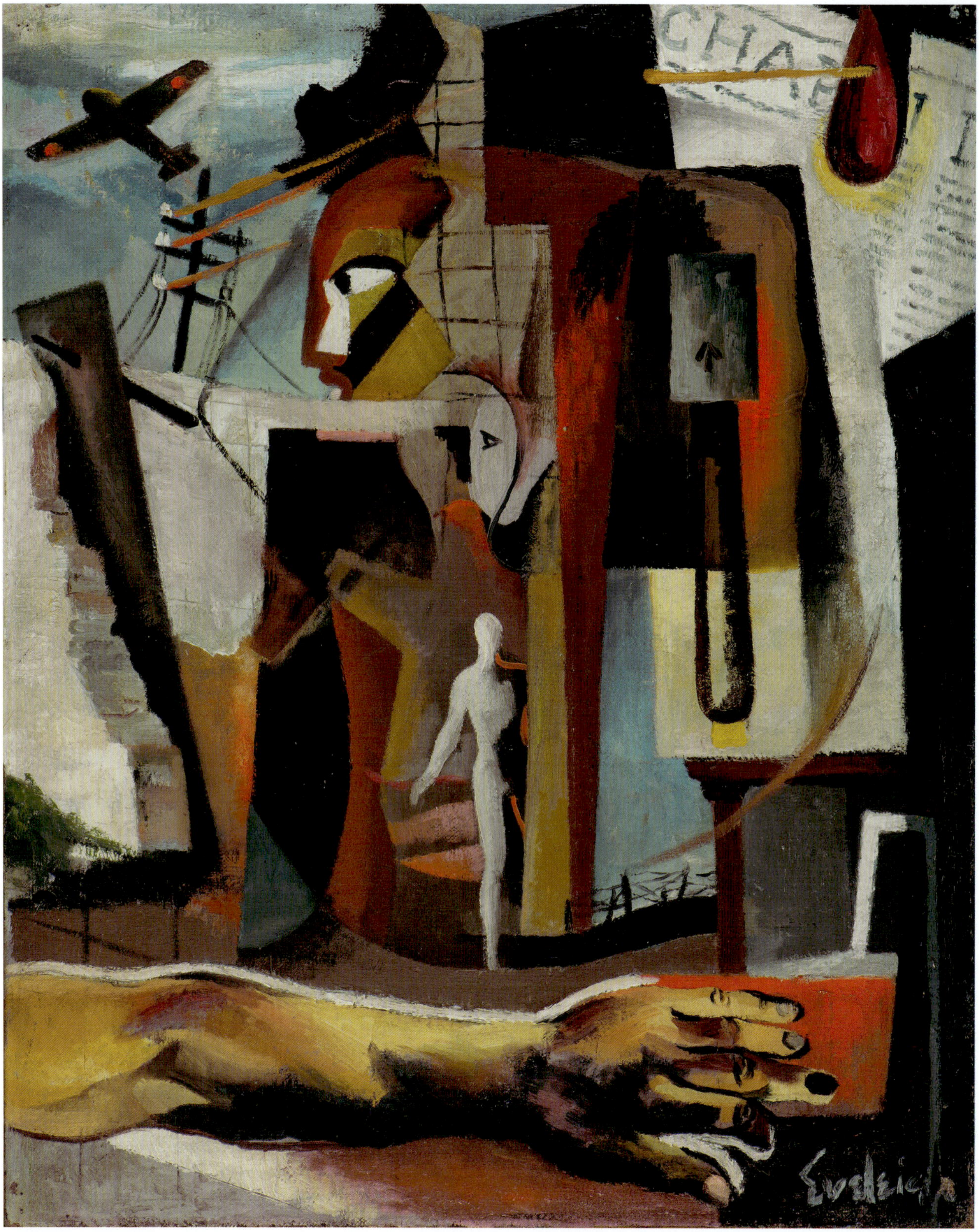

Finally, the exhibition included at least three other works – *First Air-Raid*, *Skies over England*, and *Chapel* – whose elements also seem to have been composed using an assemblage technique, but which touched critics on another level, since they were on the subject of war.

None of the works featured on the list for the 1942 exhibition bears the evocative title *War Commentary*, which is that of the remarkable painting belonging to the Montreal Museum of Fine Arts. The complex composition of this work juxtaposes three distinct spaces. One, structured like a "collage," consists of areas of colour in which are embedded various motifs that are simultaneously Synthetic Cubist and Surrealist in spirit: a newspaper cutting, what could be a bomb, a Cubist-style human profile, and a ghost-like figure hovering behind a white mannequin, all set among geometric forms that vaguely suggest some kind of building closed off on the extreme left by a half-ruined wall. At the bottom of the image, a huge and apparently unattached arm lies on the ground. Finally, behind this radically modern conflation, a more realistic section shows a bomber traversing a grey sky and a telegraph pole with its attendant wires. As there are no references to a work titled *War Commentary* in exhibition lists from this period, nor in any reviews, it seems reasonable to wonder whether this painting may have been exhibited under another title. My most recent investigations into this question are summarized in the sidebar "*War Commentary*: Questions and Conjectures."

In concluding this section on the positive critical reception accorded Eveleigh's 1942 exhibition – which saw him described as "one of our most individual and intelligent artists" (Jean-Charles Harvey)[70] and which characterized the show as an "interesting and provocative" display (Dorothy Sangster),[71] confirming that Eveleigh's painting had henceforth to be "taken into account" (Charles Doyon)[72] – I must discuss one last work: *Emotion*. Charles Doyon was alone in mentioning this gestural abstraction. His remarks were brief and interrogative: "Embryo or nebula? What is the point of this strawberry and vermilion whirlwind in a swirl of saffron waves, framed by a brownish trail, that the artist calls *Emotion*?"[73]

ill. 47 – p. 102
Henry Eveleigh
War Commentary, about 1938–39

In order to measure the originality of this example of gestural abstraction, about which the critics said virtually nothing, it should be noted that two of them, Charles Doyon and Jean-Charles Harvey, attempted in their reviews to situate Eveleigh in relation to the two dominant francophone artists who, in 1942, defined the "avant-garde": Borduas and Pellan.

Harvey compared Eveleigh principally to Pellan:

> Like all the painters of the so-called revolutionary school, he destroys all the conventional frameworks, all the forms of nature, all academicisms. In this, he aligns himself with Borduas and Pellan, to the horror of the conformists. Although displaying less skill and vigour than Pellan, he nevertheless paints with greater imagination. His abstractions are less striking; but they are not less suggestive, and they offer as much scope to the powers of evocation of the uninitiated such as we.[74]

Doyon, on the other hand, who saw Eveleigh as operating "somewhere between Pellan's ideas and the theories of Borduas," considered him "less dazzling than Pellan." He saw Eveleigh's version of Surrealism as close to Dali's and less accomplished than Borduas's, which, for Doyon, was "an unequivocal success."[75]

In retrospect, it may seem surprising that Doyon failed to make the connection between the gestural abstraction of *Emotion*, which aimed to translate the artist's inner vision, and another expressive form of "sur-realism." It seems that in 1942 the only examples of Eveleigh's work the critics associated with Surrealism were those that, like Dali's, were composed of an assemblage of relatively recognizable motifs. But perhaps, against the backdrop of 1942 Quebec, it is not remarkable that *Emotion* attracted so little attention, since its formal vocabulary was entirely driven by colour and a gesturality quite foreign to Cubism and the current conception of Surrealism. Gestural automatism as it is understood today was still in its infancy. Aside from one or two hardly seen works by Borduas,[76] it had not come to public attention until the exhibition organized by Maurice Gagnon and held in the lobby of L'Ermitage from 25 April to 2 May 1942 – a show whose invitation, in my view justifiably, bore the title "Surrealist works."[77]

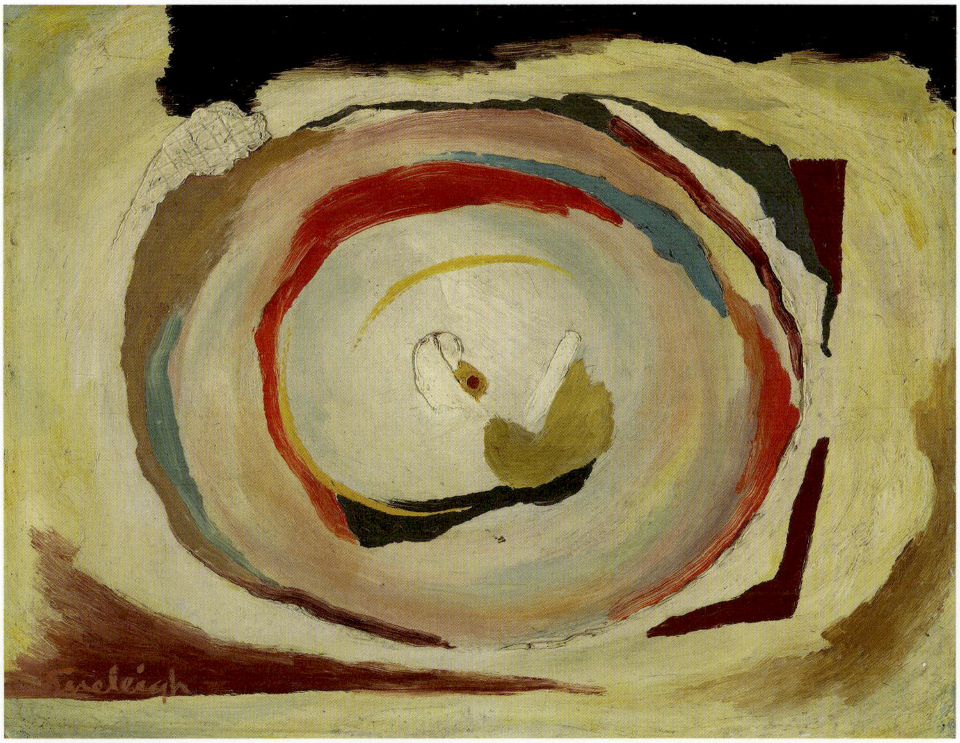

It is understandable, then, that Doyon was unable to associate Eveleigh's Surrealism with Borduas's. Borduas was a master of automatic pictorial writing (inspired by Surrealism), as witness the gouaches he exhibited in 1942. But *Emotion* represented something still relatively new on the Montreal scene: a translation in the language of non-objective gestural abstraction of an inner experience – an emotion.

Eveleigh would pursue his exploration of gestural abstraction inspired by affective states until the end of the 1940s, but parallel to the development of Automatisme.

ill. 48
Henry Eveleigh
Emotion No. 2, about 1942

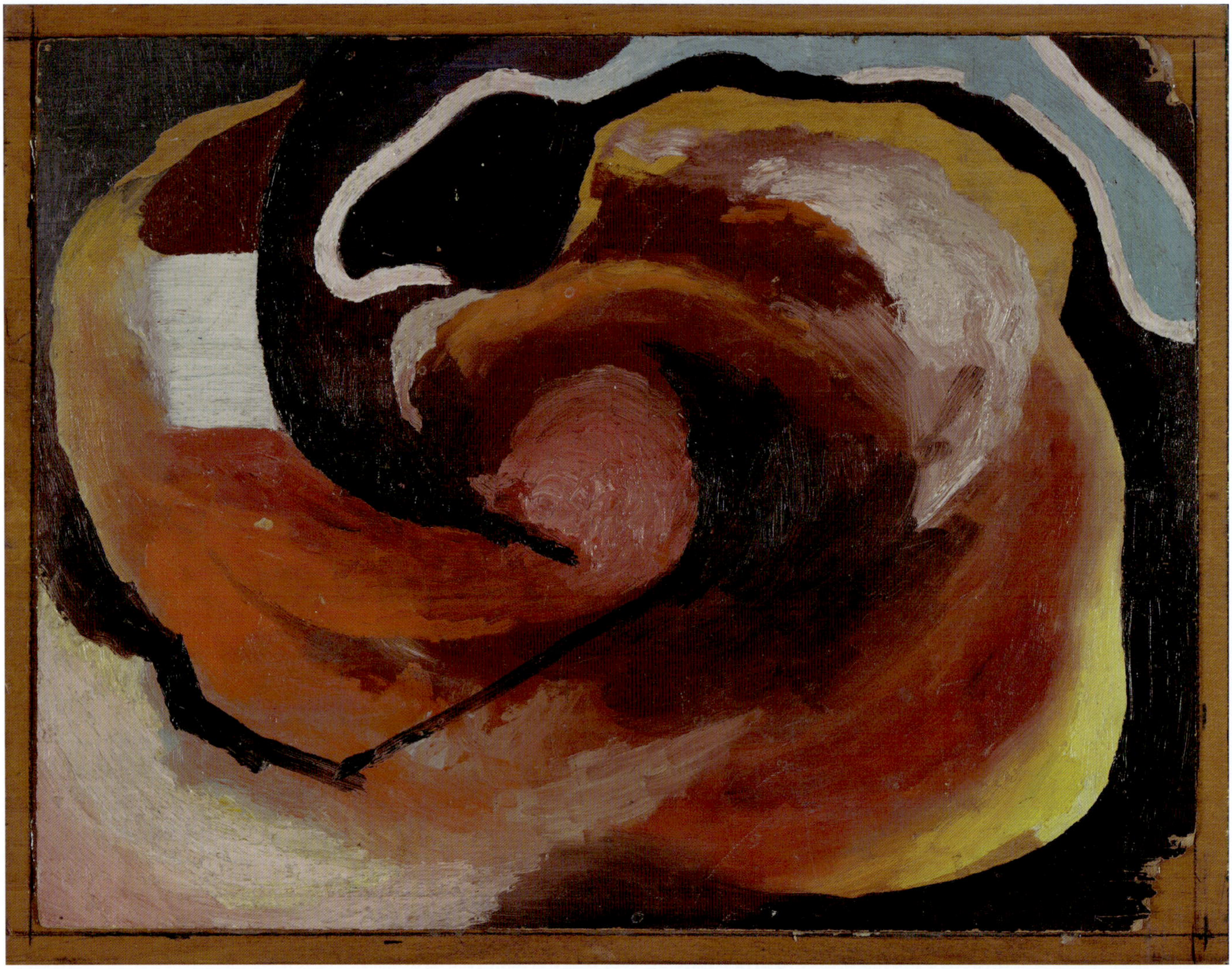

ill. 49
Henry Eveleigh
Untitled, about 1942

From Painting to Graphic Design

For Eveleigh, the 1942 exhibition at the Art Association of Montreal undoubtedly represented a high point in terms of critical reception. In the years to come, references to his work would be briefer. His contributions to the Contemporary Arts Society show of 1943 did not impress Paul Joyal (pseudonym of Gilles Hénault), who declared that Eveleigh's abstractions "came within a hair's breadth" of academicism, however paradoxical that might appear. "Tricks, techniques, formulas – it's all there," he wrote. "I do not believe that an abstraction is necessarily beautiful in itself."[78] The reviewer for the *Montreal Daily Star* offered nothing but a general description of the paintings on view: "Abstractions or pictures which approach abstractions are shown by Henry Eveleigh, P.E. Borduas, Lucien Morin, and Léon Bellefleur."[79]

Eveleigh took part in the exhibition *Aspects of Contemporary Painting in Canada*, which opened in 1943 in Andover, Massachusetts, and after a US tour concluded in 1944 at the National Gallery of Canada. In 1944 and 1946, he exhibited again with the Contemporary Arts Society, and he also participated in the two exhibitions devoted to abstract art mentioned earlier: the *Exhibition of Non-objective Paintings by Fritz Brandtner, Henry Eveleigh, and Gordon Webber*, held in Montreal, and *Excursion in Abstract*, in Toronto. There is no doubt that some of the works Eveleigh presented in these exhibitions (e.g., ill. 50) were in the same vein as *Emotion*, shown at the Art Association in 1942. This is clear from various critics' comments: "Mr. Eveleigh has a liking for whirlwinds and eddies," wrote one;[80] Eveleigh presents paintings that are "extremely emotional" declared another, "built for the most part upon a whirling circle of colour and achieving an amazing variety of mood;[81] and a third remarked, more flippantly, that Eveleigh "does many of his oils in bold sweeps of varied hues, a favoured theme being reminiscent of oysters on the half shell with what might be pearls awaiting discovery." This reviewer added: "He is the only one who clarifies his aims with such titles as 'Comment on Religion,' 'Process of Thought,' 'Study of a Pleasant Emotion,' 'Love Fugue,' 'Overture to the Sun,' 'Symphony No. 3.'"[82]

The question of titles was raised by several critics, but it was François Gagnon, writing in *La Presse*, who broached the problem of interpretation that titles could sometimes engender. "By giving titles to their canvases," he wrote, "artists are clearly encouraging us to discover their meaning." But Gagnon subscribed to a commonly held view concerning abstract works: aesthetic pleasure and individual experience could take precedence over any possible "meaning," even one suggested by a title. In any case, Gagnon concluded, many spectators make no effort to divine a meaning, "probably to maintain a sense of surprise or to take delight in spectacles not seen in nature."[83]

Meaning and the deciphering of symbols were actually subjects that recurred frequently in the writings of critics reviewing abstract art (although less so among those close to the Automatistes). And this question, of concern to so many, would often be countered by the notion that aesthetic pleasure was more important than any potential message.

After 1945, Eveleigh's reputation as a painter seems to have faded somewhat, and his name was more often associated with his work as a graphic designer – a profession he had been practising since his arrival in Montreal. During the Second World War, he designed posters for the Department of National War Services. In 1947 he won first prize in the first "Poster of the Year" contest sponsored by the United Nations (ill. 87). This prompted Roland-Hérard Charlebois (1906–1965), then director of the École des beaux-arts de Montréal, to invite Eveleigh to create a new department at the school, devoted to graphic art and design.[84]

During the postwar period, the magazine *Canadian Art* published a number of articles on the need for Canadian artists to play a role in poster design.[85] In 1947, the magazine carried a text co-written by Eveleigh and Charles Fainmel (1904–1968) – who was also a sculptor and a member of the Contemporary Arts Society – in favour of a form of progressive advertising that would not give way to the imperative: "Sell at any cost." Their position reflected a left-wing vision shared by many artists and intellectuals of the time, who aspired to a postwar world that would be more democratic, egalitarian, and just. Advertising, argued the authors, should inform, educate, and aid in the development of the highest cultural standards, while fostering good taste, health, security, good citizenship, and better understanding between peoples. It should help to make life not only fuller, but

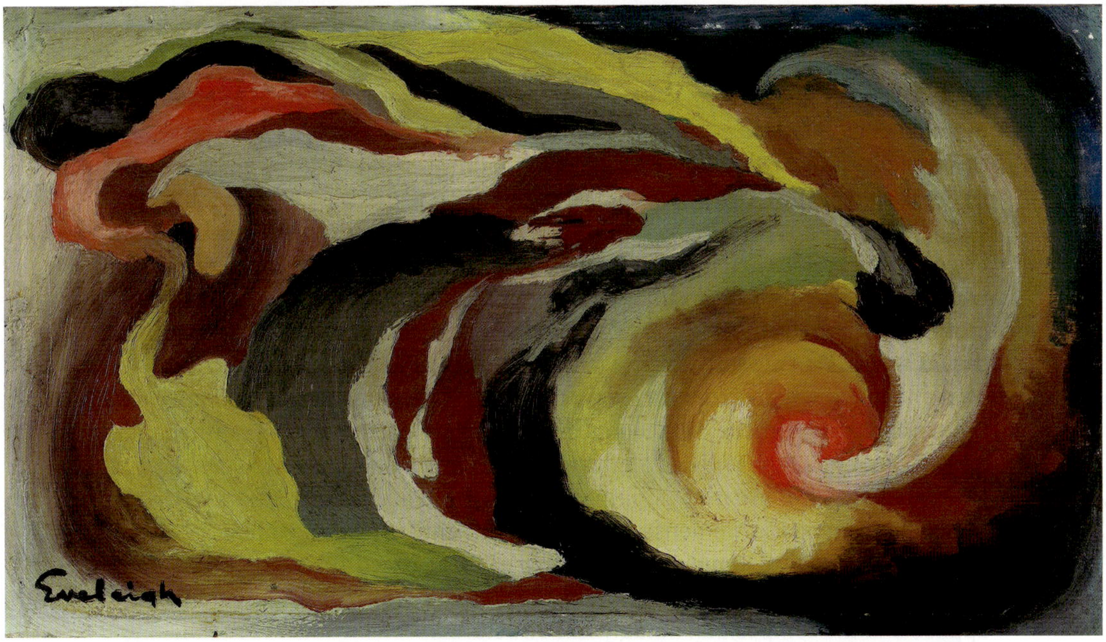

happier. And art could play a part in realizing this advertising ideal: "The research artist (the easel painter) prepares the ground for the visual trends of tomorrow, and so he should be consulted and utilized in the advertising field today."[86]

In 1947, in partnership with the graphic designer Carl Dair (1912–1967), Eveleigh founded an advertising and commercial art firm called the Eveleigh-Dair Studio, which remained in operation until 1951. In 1948 Carl Dair,[87] who also exhibited his work as a "typographical artist,"[88] published an article in *Canadian Art* on the creative possibilities of typography and the resistance to change that continued to pervade printing design in Canada. Dair nonetheless concluded his critique on a positive note by reporting the existence of Canadian schools that were disseminating a new conception of the principles of modern graphic design. He spoke particularly of exercises in "typographical abstraction" aimed at making students aware of all the elements that must be taken into account when creating visual compositions on a two-dimensional printing surface, including the texture

ill. 50
Henry Eveleigh
Emotion No. 6, 1945

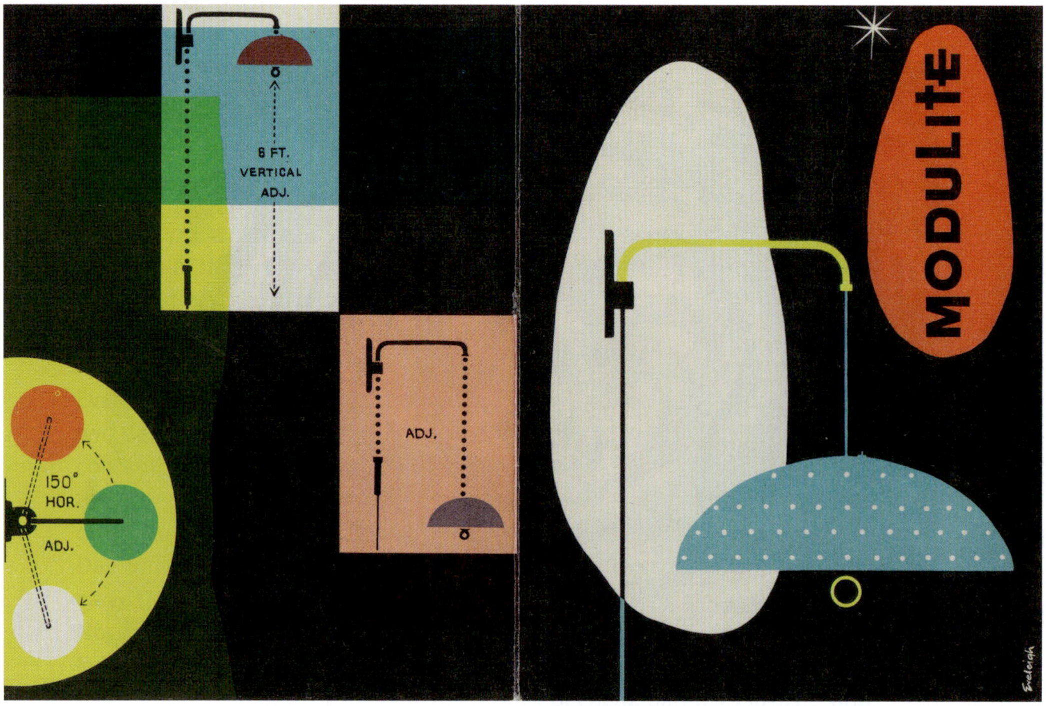

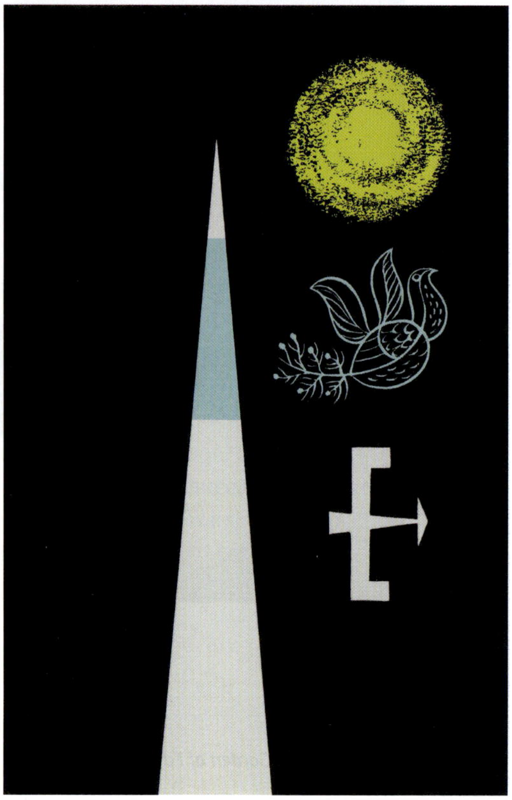

ill. 54 (*above*)
Henry Eveleigh
"Modulite" leaflet, 1955

ill. 53 (*right*)
Henry Eveleigh
Henry Eveleigh design firm leaflet, about 1955

ill. 55 (*opposite, top*)
Henry Eveleigh
"Whitehouse Industries" brochure, 1954

ill. 56 (*opposite, bottom*)
Henry Eveleigh
"Chiriotto Lodge, Ste-Adèle-en-Haut" leaflet, about 1950

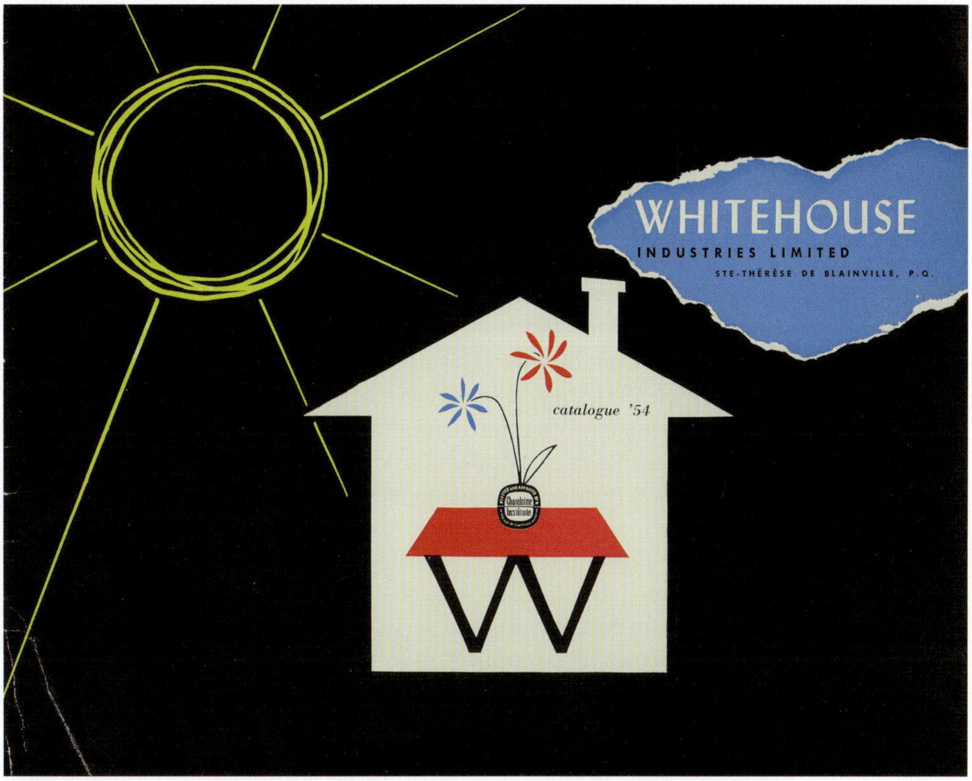
WHITEHOUSE
INDUSTRIES LIMITED
STE-THÉRÈSE DE BLAINVILLE, P.Q.
catalogue '54
Chatelaine Institute

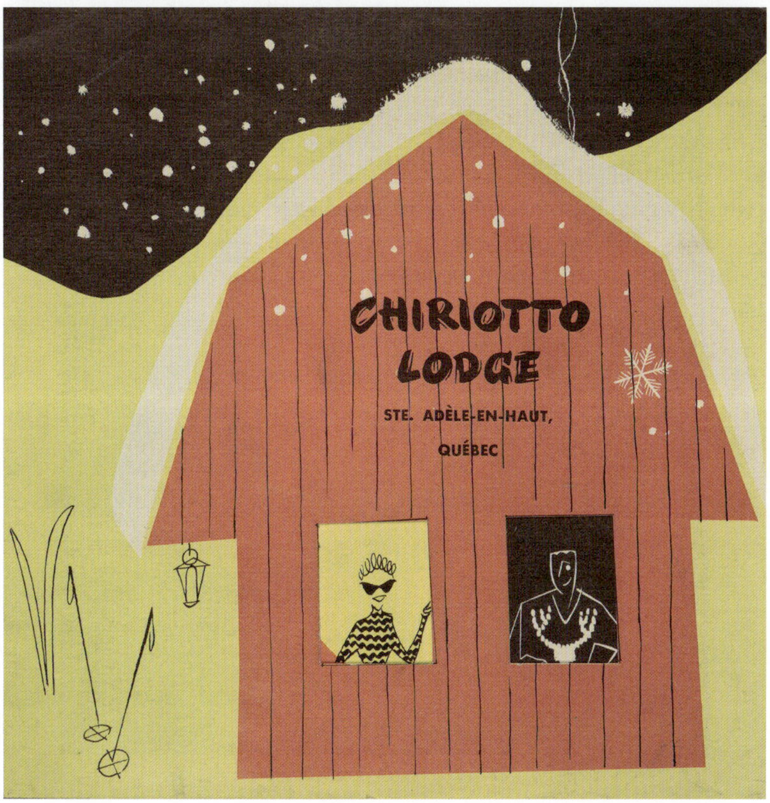
CHIRIOTTO
LODGE
STE. ADÈLE-EN-HAUT,
QUÉBEC

In the 1950 interview with Maurice Huot, Eveleigh also declared that he did not believe that artists should be obliged to live in poverty. This undoubtedly explains why he henceforth dedicated himself principally to his teaching career and his work as a graphic designer, not exhibiting his paintings again until the 1980s. In the text written for the 1981 show at UQAM, Eveleigh explained: "By 1950, to all intent and purpose, I no longer expressed myself through painting. I had become wholly engrossed with my efforts to establish Design as a practical philosophy and attitude in a somewhat hostile milieu inhabited by the advertising fraternity."

Since it is not possible to present paintings executed by Eveleigh later in the 1950s, as for the three other artists, I have chosen to briefly discuss a few examples of his advertising design work, starting with a promotional brochure for his own firm (ill. 53), which he ran from 1955 to 1962 while also working as a teacher. It shows the company logo alongside a small drawing of a dove with an olive branch. The large areas of black and white contrasting with bright colours, like yellow and blue, also appear in one of the advertising brochures he designed for the lamp and light-fixture company Modulite, which combines biomorphic forms (in the spirit of the decorative arts of the period) with brightly coloured rectangular cut-outs (ill. 54). Finally, a brochure produced for Whitehouse Industries Limited (ill. 55) and a leaflet for the Chiriotto Lodge hotel in Sainte-Adèle (ill. 56) are notable for the obvious influence of child art. In both, the contrast between black and vivid colour, again in evidence, highlights the coloured linearity of a simplified image that recalls child art, which – like naive art – inspired a whole generation of modern artists, who were drawn to its spontaneity, authenticity, and lack of formal perspective. In his work as a graphic designer, Eveleigh clearly remained connected to the artistic preoccupations of the day.

Gordon Webber

Gordon Webber, a native of Ontario, is one of the many Canadian artists whose career has yet to be fully researched. But even a partial exploration of his work, as here, reveals that he was a creator of remarkable multidisciplinarity. A painter, he was also passionately interested in photography[95] and film. Inspired by Norman McLaren (1914–1987), he created – apparently in the late 1940s – a short animated film by painting abstract forms directly on film stock.[96] Concerned with the question of the integration of art and design into modern architecture, a music lover, deeply interested in science, he also became involved in creating for the performing arts – both theatre and dance. As well as being a dedicated teacher of both adults and children, he designed his own clothes (following the example of Johannes Itten, one of the first instructors to join the Weimar Bauhaus in 1919), creating colourful, unconventional garments that aimed to conceal as far as possible his physical deformities resulting from spina bifida.[97]

It might be assumed that Webber's openness to different forms of art was the result of his studies between 1937 and 1942 at The New Bauhaus: American School of Design (which would become the Chicago School of Design in 1939), but in fact this predisposition was already evident during his years of training in Toronto. After studying at the Ontario College of Art from 1924 to 1927, he was active as a student and associate member (1927–30)[98] in the Toronto Art Students' League, which organized lectures featuring guest speakers who were not only artists, but also musicians, scientists, and philosophers. Prior to his departure for Chicago, Webber devoted time to teaching children, adults, and workers, and in 1936 and 1937 he also executed several murals.

His known painting from this period reveals the influence of the Group of Seven in its approach to landscape, while the portraits, particularly those depicting workers, are in the same spirit of social realism as those that Eveleigh and many other artists were creating during these years. Webber was also interested in music. He had apparently studied the violin,[99] and in the 1935 exhibition of the Canadian Society of Painters in Water Colour he showed two portraits of musicians, *Cello Player* and *Viola Player*. However, his most remarkable work on the subject of music is

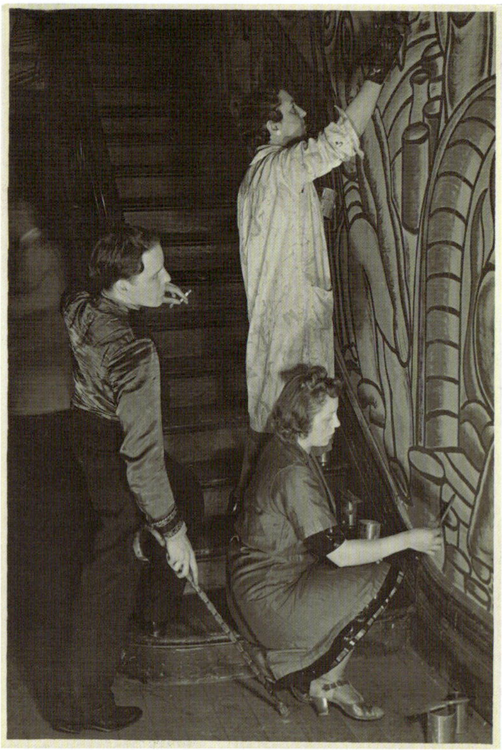

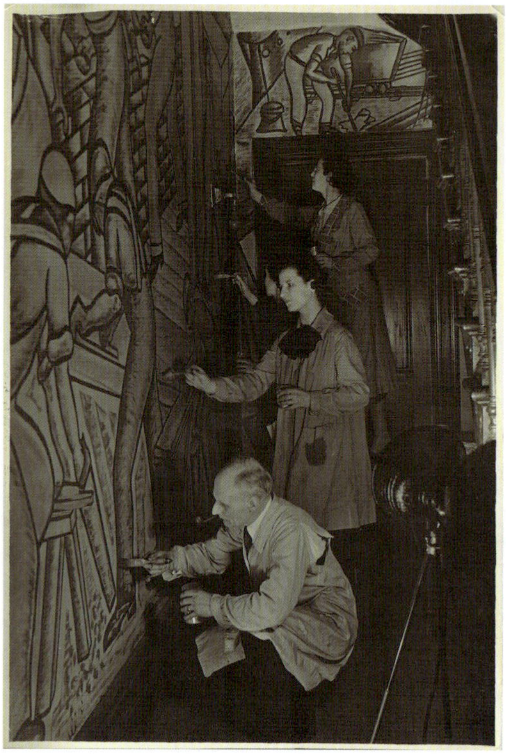

undoubtedly the *Interpretation of "Bolero" by Ravel*. Rendered in a palette whose tones conjure the earth of Spain, the work is composed of a tangle of semi-abstract forms that include several recognizably human figures, set within a rhythmic, expressive space. Dating from 1930, the painting is quite unlike Webber's other works from the period. But there is a possible explanation for its timing: Maurice Ravel composed his ballet *Bolero* in the summer of 1928, and the premiere took place a few months later, on 23 November, at the Opéra de Paris. That same year, the composer embarked on a North American tour that included recitals at the Margaret Eaton Hall in Toronto and the Théâtre Saint-Denis in Montreal. Webber could well have attended one of these events. Whatever the case, *Bolero* served as the inspiration for a painting whose rhythm and repetitions of movement and form convey all the qualities of a musical tempo.

ill. 57 (*left*) *Photograph of the execution of Gordon Webber's mural for the Workers Educational Association Centre, St George Street, Toronto*, winter 1937–38, Gordon Webber fonds, John Bland Canadian Architecture Collection, McGill University Library, Montreal. Gordon Webber, who taught at the centre during the 1930s, appears in the photo on the left, leaning on the staircase.

ill. 58 (*right*) *Photograph of the execution of Gordon Webber's mural for the Workers Educational Association Centre, St George Street, Toronto*, winter 1937–38, Gordon Webber fonds, John Bland Canadian Architecture Collection, McGill University Library, Montreal.

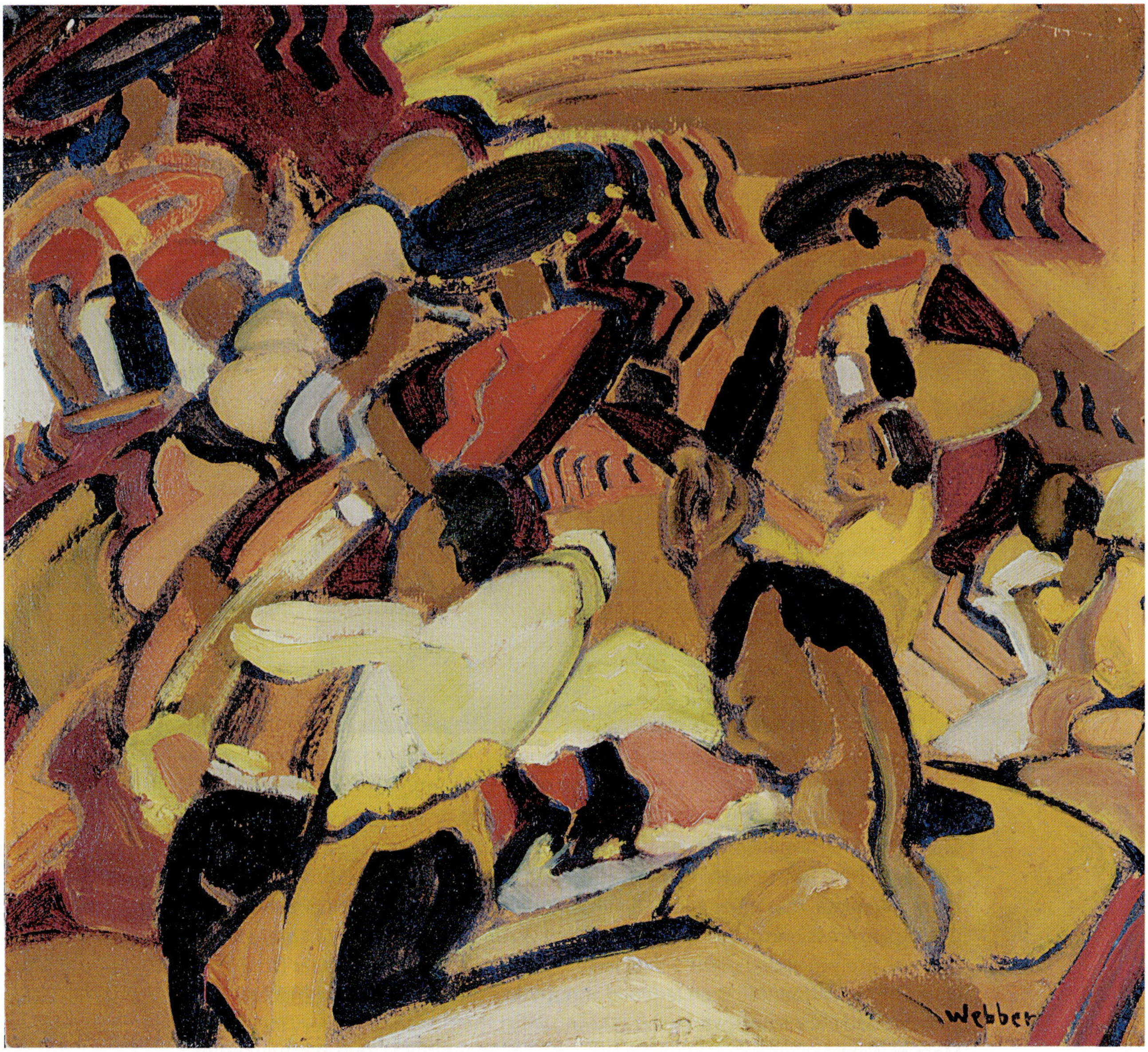

ill. 59
Gordon Webber
Interpretation of "Bolero" by Ravel, 1930

In 1941, on the occasion of the exhibition *Colour Designs by Gordon Webber*, held from 25 January to 7 February at the Picture Loan Society,[109] Graham McInnes published an article in the Toronto magazine *Saturday Night* that described Webber's approach in some detail. The critic opened by claiming that all artists are in fact abstract, in the sense that they translate their own vision and emotions in pictorial form. Speaking specifically of Webber's works, he wrote: "As abstractions, these works are pleasing. They are suave, neat, antiseptic, and the choice of tone and space relationships seems happy."[110] McInnes nevertheless admonished the artist for accompanying his works with typed texts designed to provide "keys." He refused to read them, maintaining that it is not the artist's task to give the spectator explanations, and any attempt to do so is a sign of weakness, tantamount to admitting that there is no meaning in the work – in art – only that which "arises in life." Finally, McInnes expressed the hope that the works Webber was presenting, however good, were simply a phase, and that he was not planning to follow in the footsteps of his mentor Moholy-Nagy: he should not limit himself to exquisite colour, wrote the critic, for this would shackle his emotions and his artistic possibilities. In conclusion, McInnes confessed his preference for artists like Matisse, Grosz, and Burchfield – for a more expressive approach, in other words – and described Kandinsky, Klee, Moholy-Nagy, and Feininger as "artistic vegetarians."

Abstraction and Social Critique

From what I have learned of Webber's career, the 1942–43 period seems to have constituted a distinct phase that produced a group of works integrating diverse materials (newspapers, maps, photographs) whose titles suggest a preoccupation with the social and political situation of the time.[111] Two of these works are known: *Distorted Man* and *Man's Problem*, both illustrated in an article on Webber published by Walter Abell in the June–July 1944 issue of *Canadian Art*. Abell began his text by defending the notion that an abstract or semi-abstract work can possess meaning, and that ideas can be expressed by new techniques and abstract designs. Thus transmitted, the critic maintained, they are actually "more stimulating to the modern mind than when conveyed by older and more

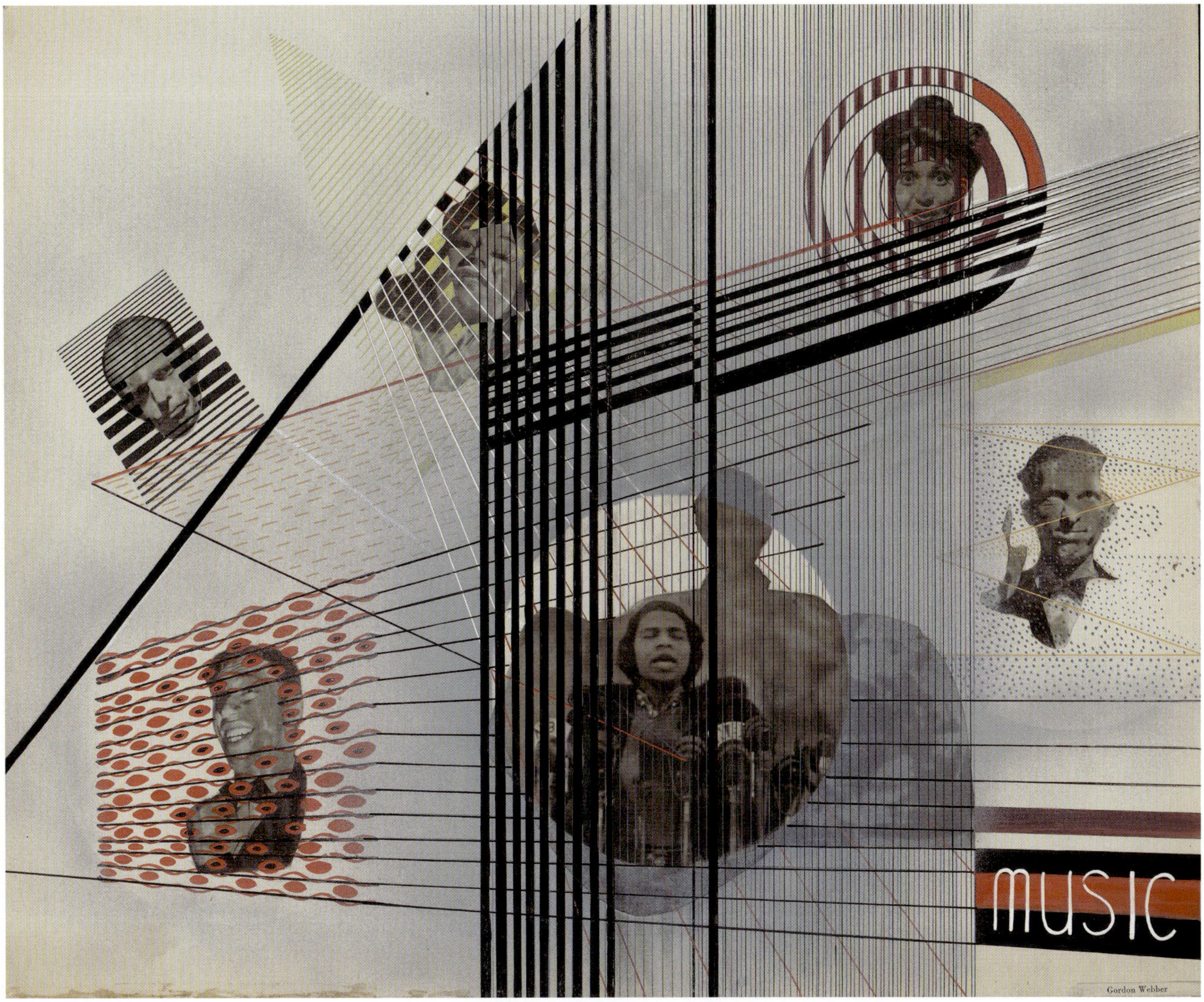

ill. 61
Gordon Webber
Music, 1942

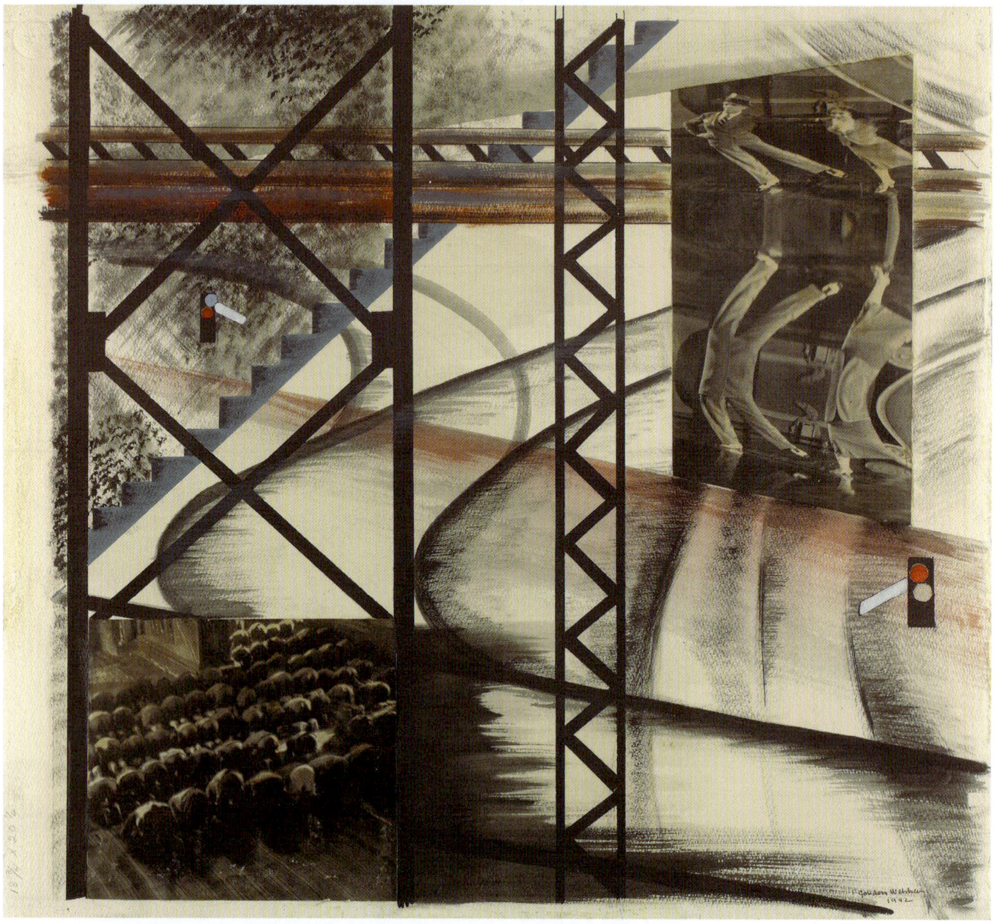

ill. 62
Gordon Webber
Distorted Man, December 1942

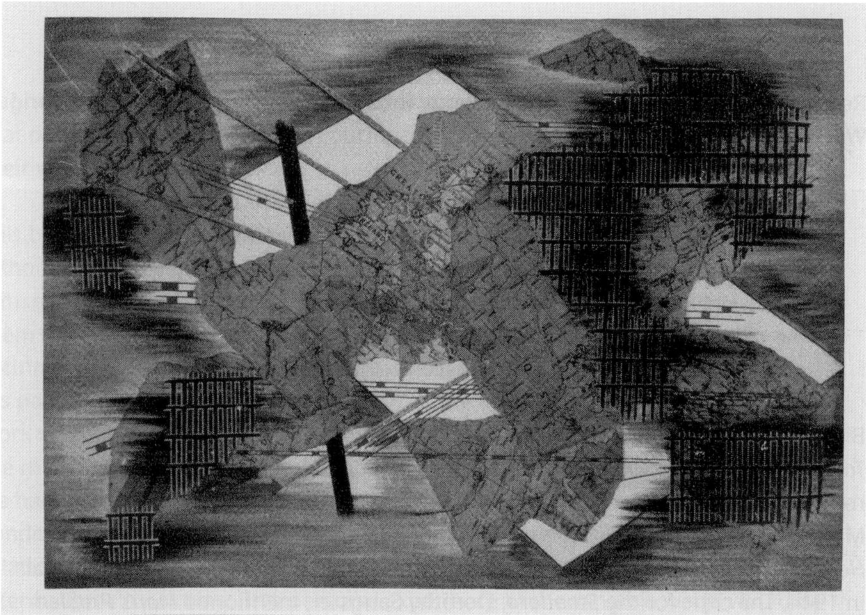

stereotyped methods."[112] Abell then cited the artist's own comments about the two works pictured. Webber said that he had composed *Distorted Man* "to express the inhuman atmosphere of big cities where little natural movement is possible." Abell then proceeded to explain the strategies the artist had employed to achieve his end:

> A geometrical framework of design conveys a feeling of the inflexibility of an urban environment. In the upper right corner, the distorted images of a man and a woman symbolize the effect of such an environment on humanity. At the lower left, rows of prostrate worshippers suggest the devotions of mankind to the false gods of ruthless mechanization.[113]

ill. 63
Gordon Webber
Man's Problem, about 1942–43
Reproduced in *Canadian Art* 1, no. 5 (June–July 1944): 201.

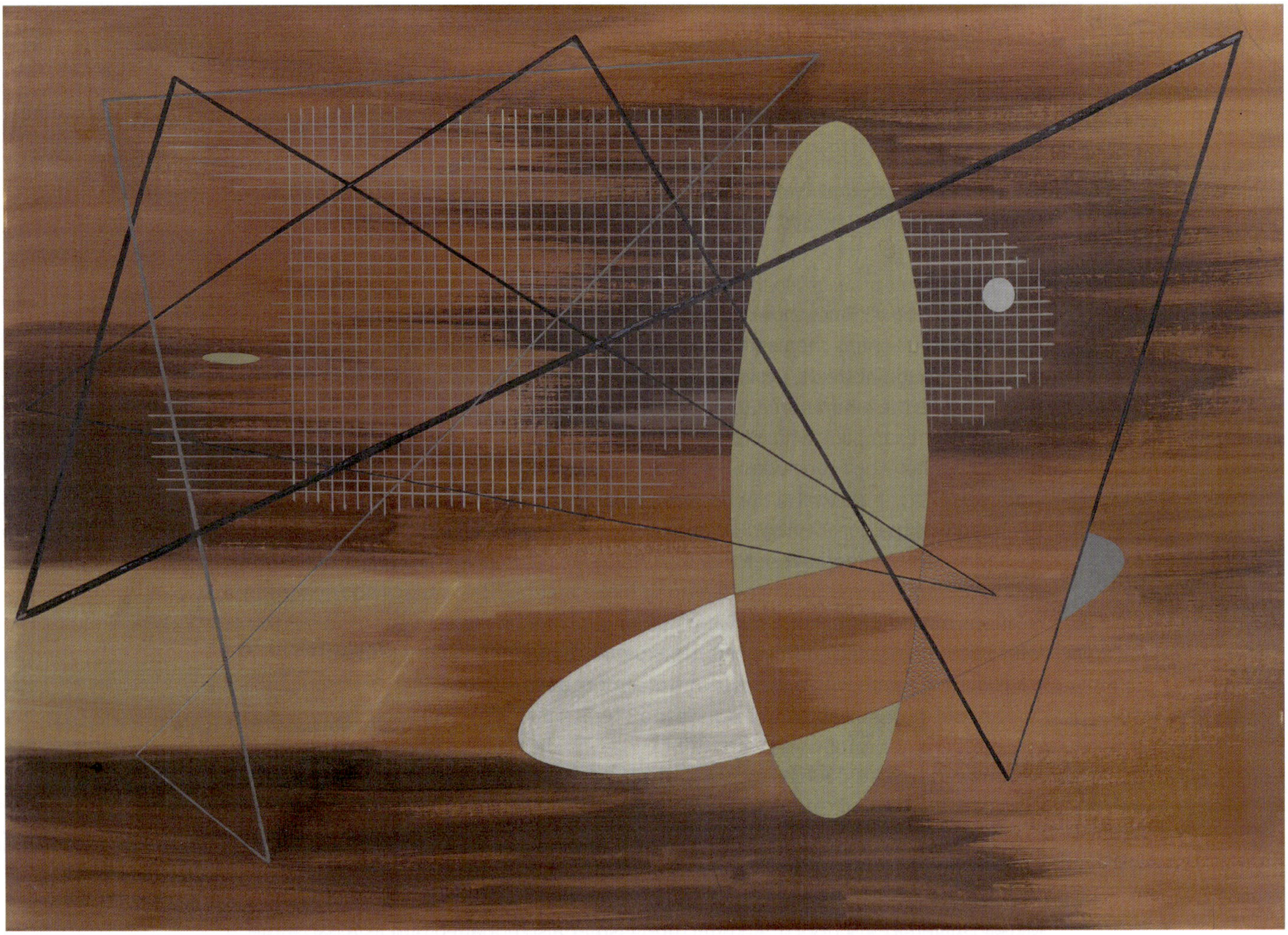

ill. 64
Gordon Webber
Design No. 1, Vermont, 1946
A label on the back of the painting indicates that it was exhibited in 1947 at the Art Association of Montreal's Spring Exhibition.

execution. He apparently started the numbering afresh each year, which means that there are works bearing the same title and the same number, but a different date. There also appears to have been a separate numbering system for different mediums, so a title like *Design No. 1* could be used to identify both a painting and a watercolour. The fact that works were sometimes exhibited or reproduced under different titles on different occasions only adds to the confusion.

The works I have selected all display basic similarities of composition and motif. Geometric or linear forms are superimposed over a background that could be described as atmospheric or landscape-like. These grounds are modulated by alternations of colour from dark to light, creating a sense of depth. In the series of *Designs*, which Webber would continue producing until the early 1950s, he overlaid the grounds with different types of motif, often including a grid form, as in *Design No. 1, Vermont* (1946), *Design No. 1, Vermont* (1947), *Design No. X*,[120] and *Abstract Composition No. 1*. In all these works, and also in *Design No. 13, Berkshires*, unbroken lines trace a closed circuit – geometric, triangular, or curved – that sometimes fills the space with coloured convolutions or ovoid shapes. In other examples, the composition is enriched by articulations of straight or diagonal lines, as in *Design No. 1, Vermont* (1947) and *Music*. In some instances, such as *Design No. 1, Vermont* (1946) and *Design No. 14, Berkshires*, the artist also employs solid forms, and in various works throughout the series, smaller filled-in circles or squares can be seen here and there.

A work belonging to the Montreal Museum of Fine Arts, *Abstract Composition (Design No. 1)* (ill. 70),[121] differs somewhat from those just mentioned, owing to the rigour of its geometric composition. It consists of a rhythmic series of square and rectangular forms, composed of grids or textured colours, which are suspended in spaces of varying depth. Within these spaces appear semi-transparent circular shapes and broad curves, probably executed with an airbrush, likely also used to create the forms in the foreground. Slightly to the right of centre, a tiny white square, haloed by dark colours but suspended in the middle of a paler area, creates a focal point. In other works from the same period, similar little circles and squares – black, white, red, or green – stand out from the overall composition and attract the gaze in much the same way. All this denotes an approach deeply concerned with questions of space, form, and geometry, with clear affiliations

It appears that for this show Webber again indulged in his practice of accompanying the works with explanatory texts concerning the "ideas" they embodied. We learn this from an article in *Le Canada* by Renée Normand, who confessed to being perplexed by Webber's contributions, which seemed to her like "charts of ideas." Defining his works as "non-figurative, 'abstract' in the simplest sense of the word," she saw them as attempts to illustrate "something odourless, colourless and, more importantly, invisible: an idea, a subjective impression." She was clearly not convinced. Admittedly, she wrote, there were always the "explanatory texts that recount in very free prose the emotion that Mr. Webber wishes to express in visual terms. For example: 'the idea bandied about in a conversation.'" But in Renée Normand's view, the "chart of an idea" can turn out to be "entirely unrelated to the usual concerns of the visual arts." Painters, she declared, "must employ the methods of the trade" – which according to her Webber failed to do – "otherwise they might as well be orators, mathematicians, grocers." She felt that his colours were "arbitrary" and "unconcerned with the values of tones," and that his geometric system ignored "basic relationships between volumes in pursuit of the recalcitrant idea."[128] Normand was evidently not a fan of geometric abstraction, and the painter's explanations did little to change her mind.

Graham McInnes had chided Webber in 1940 for his accompanying texts, arguing that it was not the artist's job to supply "keys" of interpretation, since any meaning must lie within the work itself. In my view, however, the critics' lack of understanding (possibly exacerbated by the painter's explanations) had the effect of obscuring for spectators of the time the true influence of the Bauhaus and Moholy-Nagy on Webber's pictorial practice. It was an approach based on the abstract design of the painting and an innovative use of materials, mediums, and space, all couched in a contemporary sensibility. This was undoubtedly the vision Webber was defending when, in 1942, he confided to Walter Abell that his works were inspired by his sensorial and visual experience of the world. Perhaps his only mistake was to try to also put this experience into words, instead of allowing painting to speak for itself.

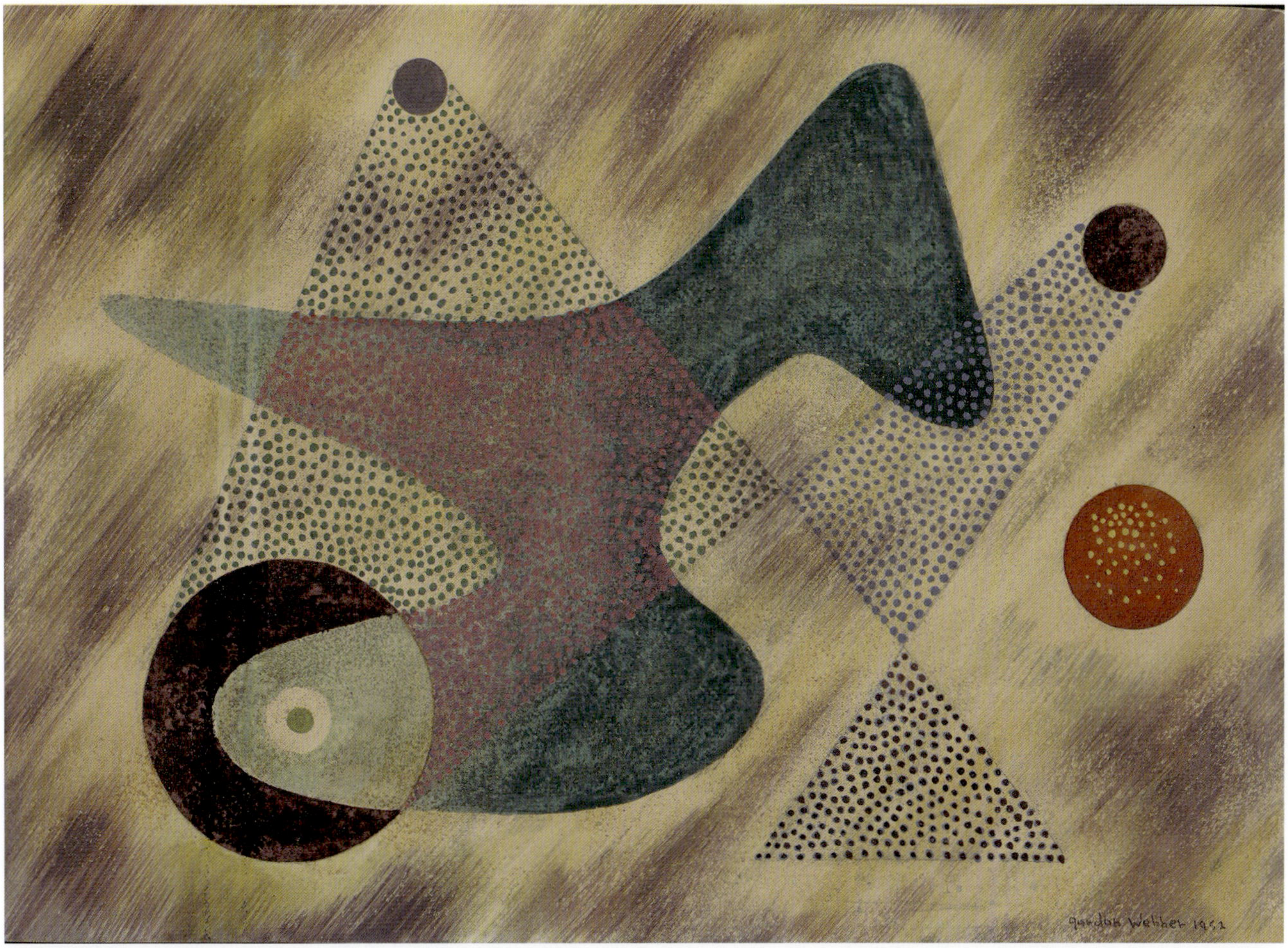

ill. 69
Gordon Webber
Design No. 14, Berkshires, 1952

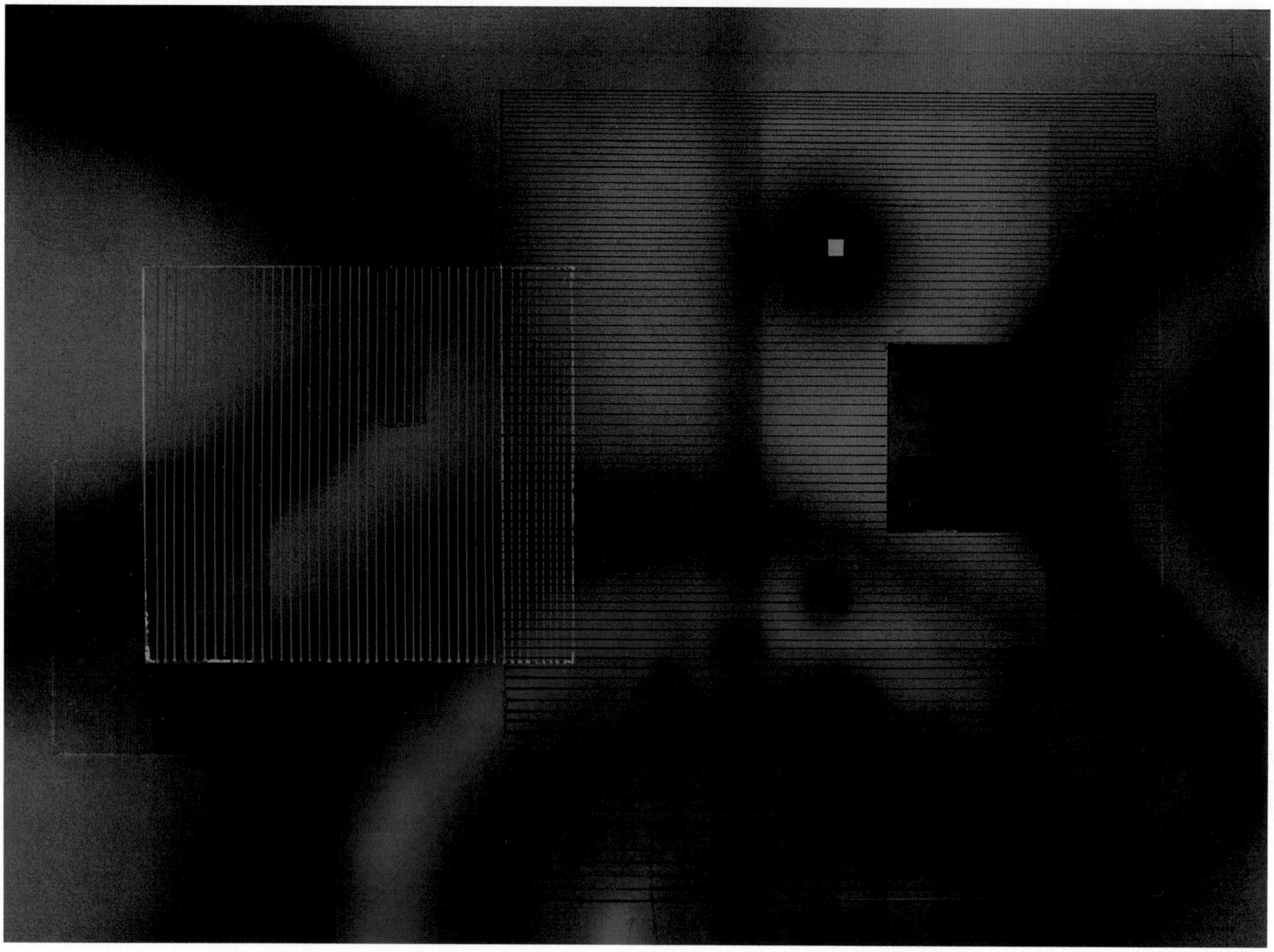

ill. 70
Gordon Webber
Abstract Composition (Design No.1), 1944

The most illuminating text on Webber's practice was published by Arthur Lismer in the October–November 1946 issue of the *Northern Review*. Lismer, a founding member of the Group of Seven, had taught the young Webber in Toronto, as well as engaging him as an instructor at his Children's Art Centre. It was also Lismer who suggested that Webber study at the New Bauhaus in Chicago, which had been founded by his friend László Moholy-Nagy.[129] Lismer's openness to the pedagogical approach that reigned at the Bauhaus explains his sympathetic attitude toward Webber's art, so very different from his own. It is worth looking at his article more closely.

After a review of the artist's early life, Lismer described his period of study at the Chicago School of Design (New Bauhaus). There, he maintained, Webber had "found what he was after, a new world of meaning, a world where design meant something, a visual language with a sound vocabulary, a basic philosophy and a foundation in architecture, and the arts of living." According to Lismer, this experience allowed Webber to break with naturalism, while remaining distinct from a particular form of European abstraction. His was a painting, wrote Lismer, devoid of both "superficial mysticism" and "European derivations."

> [His works] have no foothold in nature, in legend or history. They belong to this concrete world of movement, speed, mechanisms, and express the inarticulate ideas and experiences of modern man, who moves, works, and travels, in and through this world … In Webber's paintings [there] is a new world with thoughtful craftmanship, deliberation, and vision; the port-hole is enlarged and we step through it into an ordered existence, that puts our cluttered cities and our crowded inglorious lives to shame. It is a clean world, without gossip and superficial social ornaments, without ideologies … a world that functions with organic rhythm like a steady, beating heart.[130]

For Lismer, Webber's art was situated above (or outside of) abstraction in the strict sense, for it was inseparable from the design that produces what is best suited to life in a modern world, "a less cluttered world, stripped for constructive action, wherein science, education, technology, social forces and art can begin to create anew."

Lismer's compelling 1946 defence of the abstraction practised by Webber and of his optimistic vision of a modern world that would be organized, technological, and free of disorder seems to have been another expression of the utopian yearning for a better future experienced by so many artists and intellectuals in the postwar years.

A Glimpse of the 1950s

Webber continued to exhibit his work during the 1950s, notably with the Canadian Group of Painters, at the Montreal Museum of Fine Arts' annual Spring Exhibitions and as a member of the Non-Figurative Artists' Association of Montréal, founded in 1956. At the start of the decade his works were still being titled *Design*, followed by a number and the year, often accompanied by a reference to location (e.g., *Design No. 14*, *Berkshires*). From the middle of the 1950s on, however, exhibition catalogues began listing titles like *Abstract Composition*, often – although not always – followed by a number and a place name (e.g., Mexico, Hamburg, Berkshires).

Abstract Composition from 1952 warrants a few words. In the research file prepared prior to the work's acquisition by the Montreal Museum of Fine Arts in 1996, the curator, Rosalind Pepall, judiciously noted: "The optical effects of forms, lines, dots, small areas of bright colour and movement within a confined space all point to Webber's debt to his teacher Moholy-Nagy and to his knowledge of the work of Paul Klee, whom he admired."

Like *Abstract Composition* from 1954, the painting echoes earlier works: it again features an atmospheric background of shifting light and dark areas, over which are superimposed geometric forms highlighted here and there with decorative motifs that establish a rhythm and increase the perceptual complexity of the various volumes and spaces. Another constant is the artist's evident interest in the textures offered by different materials – in this case the sand that has been added to the surface.

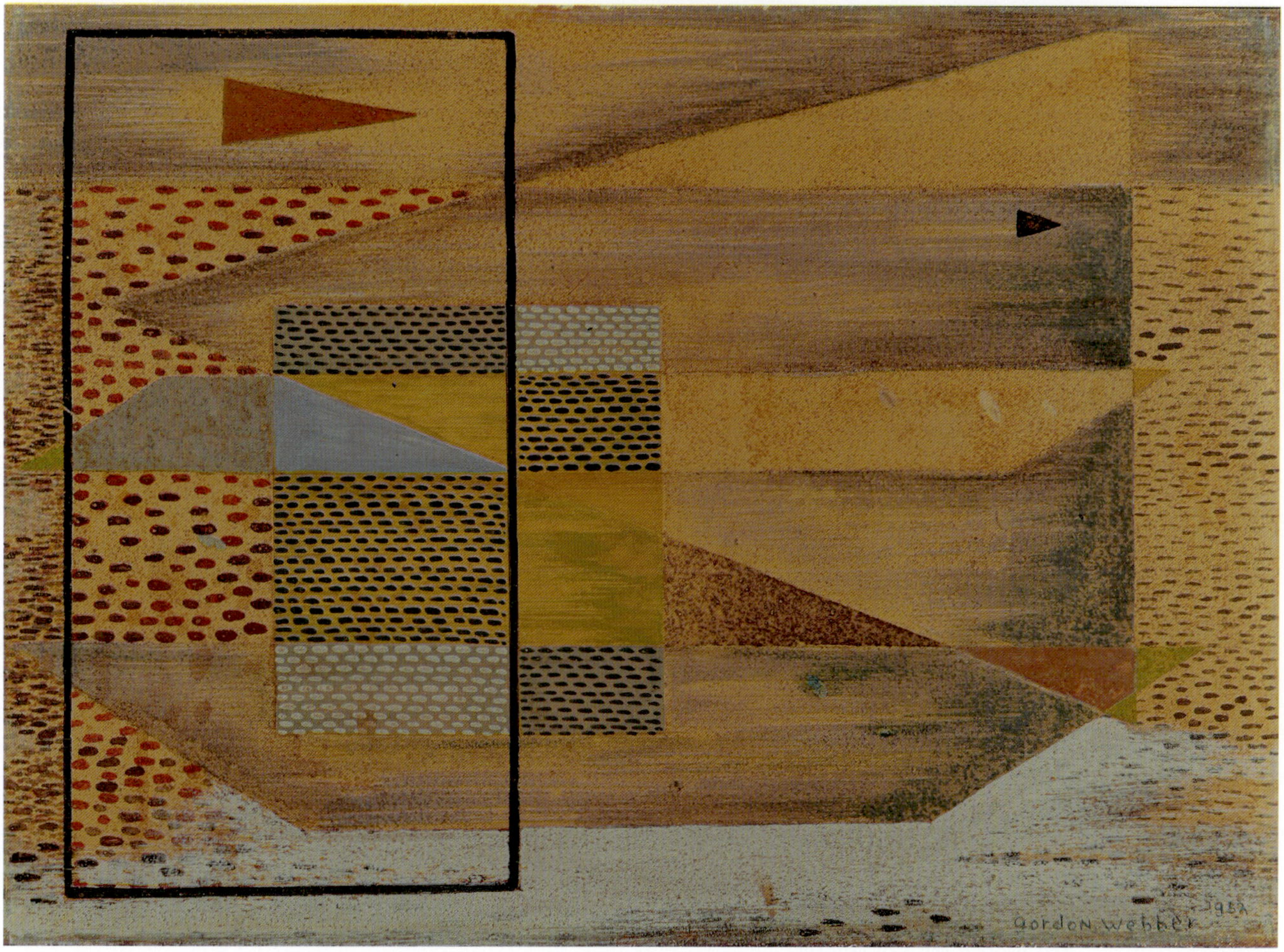

ill. 71
Gordon Webber
Abstract Composition, 1952

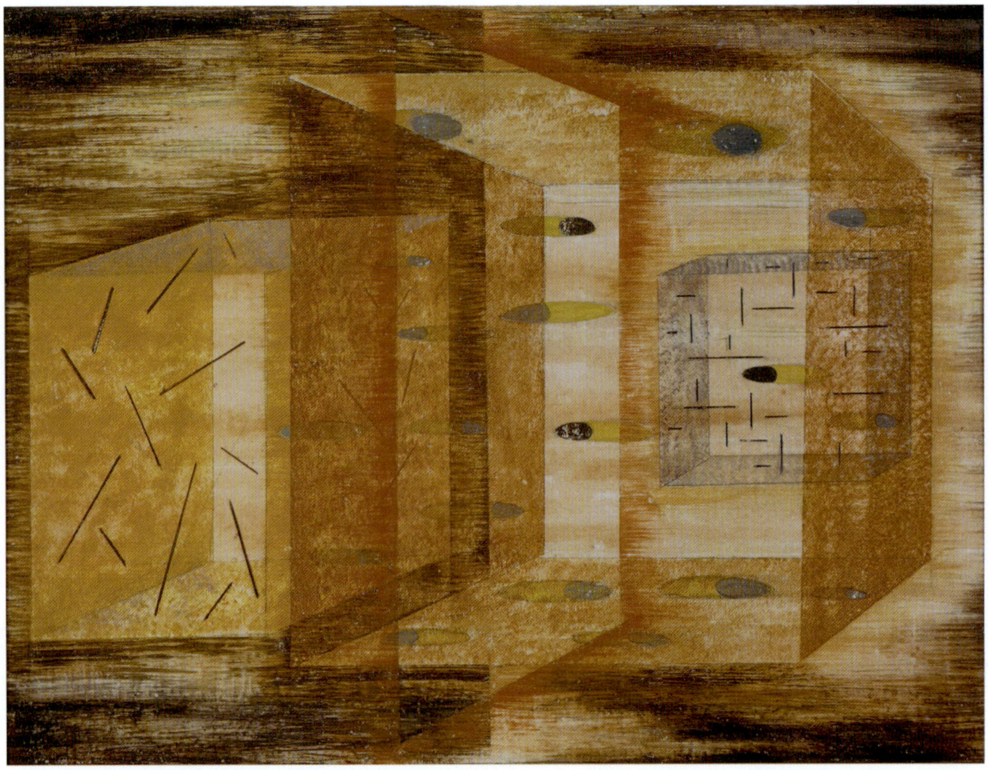

Toward the end of the 1950s, the artist produced a series of works whose title, *Incident*, was again accompanied by a geographical location. In the second of two examples, *Incident, Michigan* and *Incident, Washington*, the artist abandoned the atmospheric ground: instead, powerful diagonals cross the picture plane, creating triangular forms whose surfaces are entirely covered with small, juxtaposed dabs of colour.

ill. 72
Gordon Webber
Abstract Composition, 1954

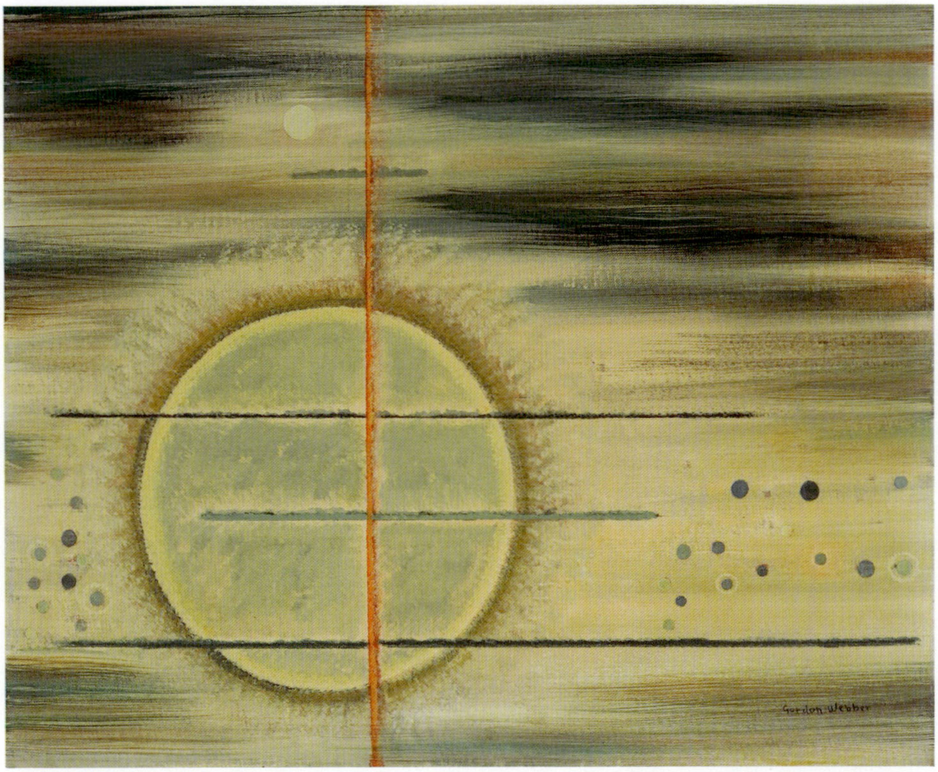

Webber would continue experimenting and developing his approach, exploring the rhythm of geometrical forms in greater depth and sometimes introducing references to traffic – as in the 1957 work *On Highway #64* (The Montreal Museum of Fine Arts). This latter device added another dimension to the notion of travel already suggested by the geographical component of certain titles. By the 1960s, he was even occasionally introducing figurative elements that, though rendered semi-abstractly, are nonetheless easily identifiable. Examples of such works include *Delos Antiquity* (1964; location unknown), *Aegean Island of Silver VII* (n.d.; McGill University Visual Arts Collection, Montreal), and *Abstracted Hills* (1960; location unknown).

ill. 73
Gordon Webber
Incident, Michigan, 1957–59

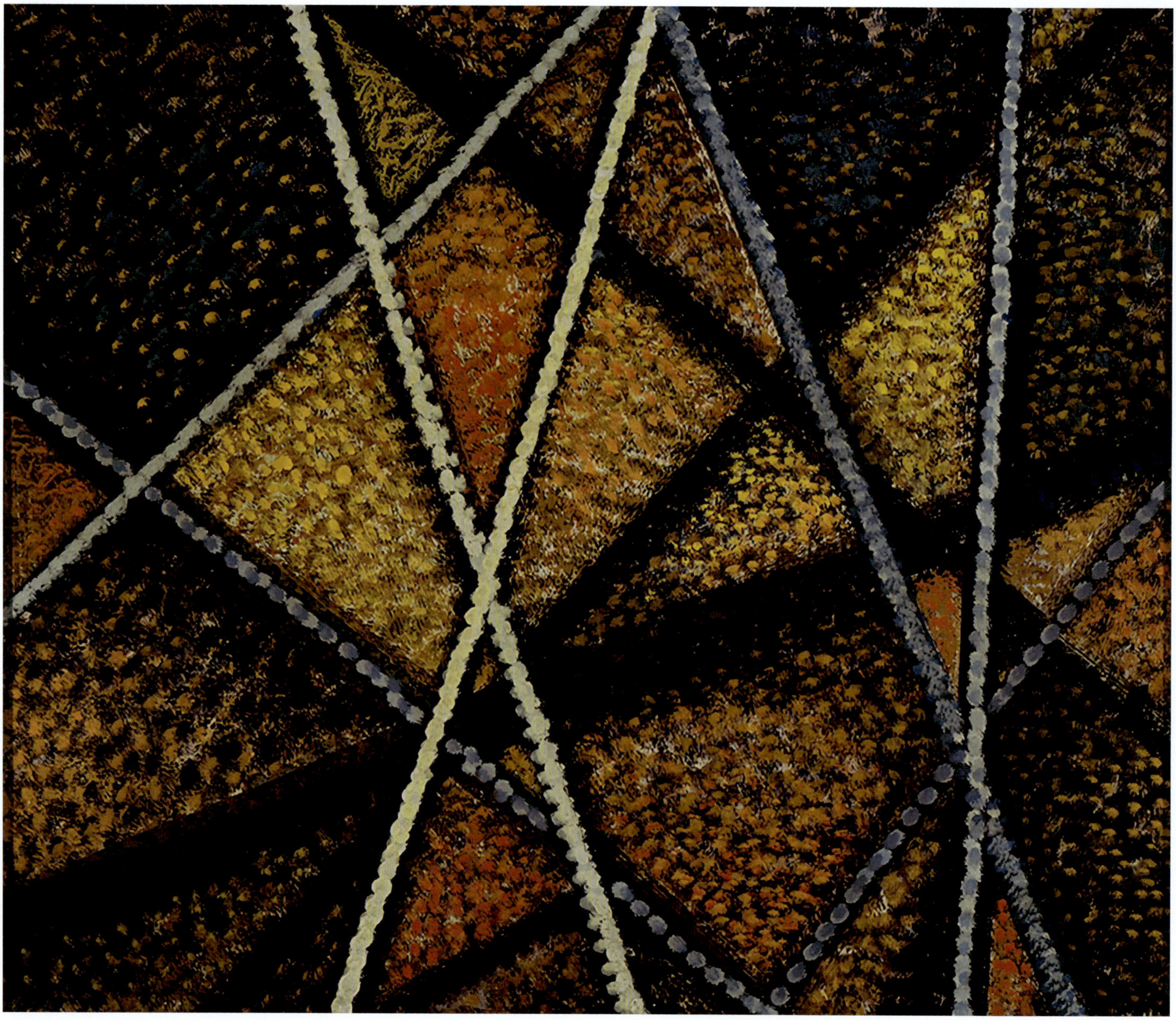

ill. 74
Gordon Webber
Incident, Washington, 1959

So What Did It Mean, Abstraction?

It is not easy to summarize in all its complexity the notion of abstraction as understood by critics in the 1940s. First, though, it is important to note that an attitude of moral judgment that was common during the 1930s – the idea that modern art, particularly abstraction and Surrealism, was the product of a decadent society and a decline in values – had disappeared. The focus had shifted toward the question of "meaning," of the intelligibility of a work. What could critics and spectators hope to "understand"? In view of the multiple definitions assigned to the word "abstraction" throughout the decade, there are several possible answers to this question.

Critics rarely took exception to so-called abstract works that were based on "identifiable" forms (a nude, a portrait, an urban scene, a landscape – even images of atoms and cells, as in certain works by Brandtner, Eveleigh, and Scott), and they were apparently prepared to appreciate (or not) the formal innovations the artists had employed in presenting their personal vision of a subject. Things become more complicated when the juxtaposition of sometimes individually identifiable motifs (a hand, a tree, an arm, a human figure) was guided by the "logic" of Surrealism, creating a "narrative" whose meaning was not clear to the spectator. In these cases, critics tended to stress the poetic dimension of the work, seeing it as an expression of the artist's own dream, desire, or imagination, to which spectators did not necessarily have access. This did not prevent a few critics from trying their hand at interpretation, notably, as we have seen, with Eveleigh's works.

When the expression of the creator's inner world was manifested in a version of gestural abstraction, without any reference to the tangible world – as in Eveleigh's *Emotions* series, and even more obviously in paintings by the Automatistes – critics, aside from a few initiates, hardly knew how to react, except by noting the brilliance of the works, their chromatic richness, the dynamism of their movement and forms. Which brings us to a third position. According to this view, a painting was not required to "mean" anything, and abstraction could be, like music, a "pure" form of expression. In the appreciation of "pure painting," nothing was to be taken into account aside from the work's formal elements – their arrangement and the dynamic they created on the pictorial surface. The pleasure experienced by spectators did not arise from their "understanding" of some narrative or other, but from the purely visual and sensorial enjoyment to be derived from contemplation of the work. Needless to say, this view of non-objective or non-figurative art was not unanimously endorsed during the 1940s. Although gestural works, seen as an expression of the artist's inner world, seem to have been accepted relatively easily, when it came to more geometric, formalist, creations – like a number of Gordon Webber's paintings, for example – many critics balked. In fact, it would not be until the 1950s that geometric abstraction would flourish and gain recognition, largely under the impetus of the Plasticien movement. It would also be during this period that the notion of abstraction would be consistently linked to non-objectivity. But that is a whole other story.

—

I shall return in the conclusion of this study to the particularities of the practices of these four artists. As regards their overall contribution, however, there is another aspect of their work that must be underscored and that largely distinguishes them from their francophone counterparts: the role they played in a broader reflection on the social function of art. This will be the subject of the next chapter, which, while focused on the social and political situation of the time, will also look at the diversity of the aesthetic ideas and approaches that coexisted on the Montreal arts scene during the 1940s.

Gordon Webber
Design No. X (detail), 1948–49
ill. 66, page 129

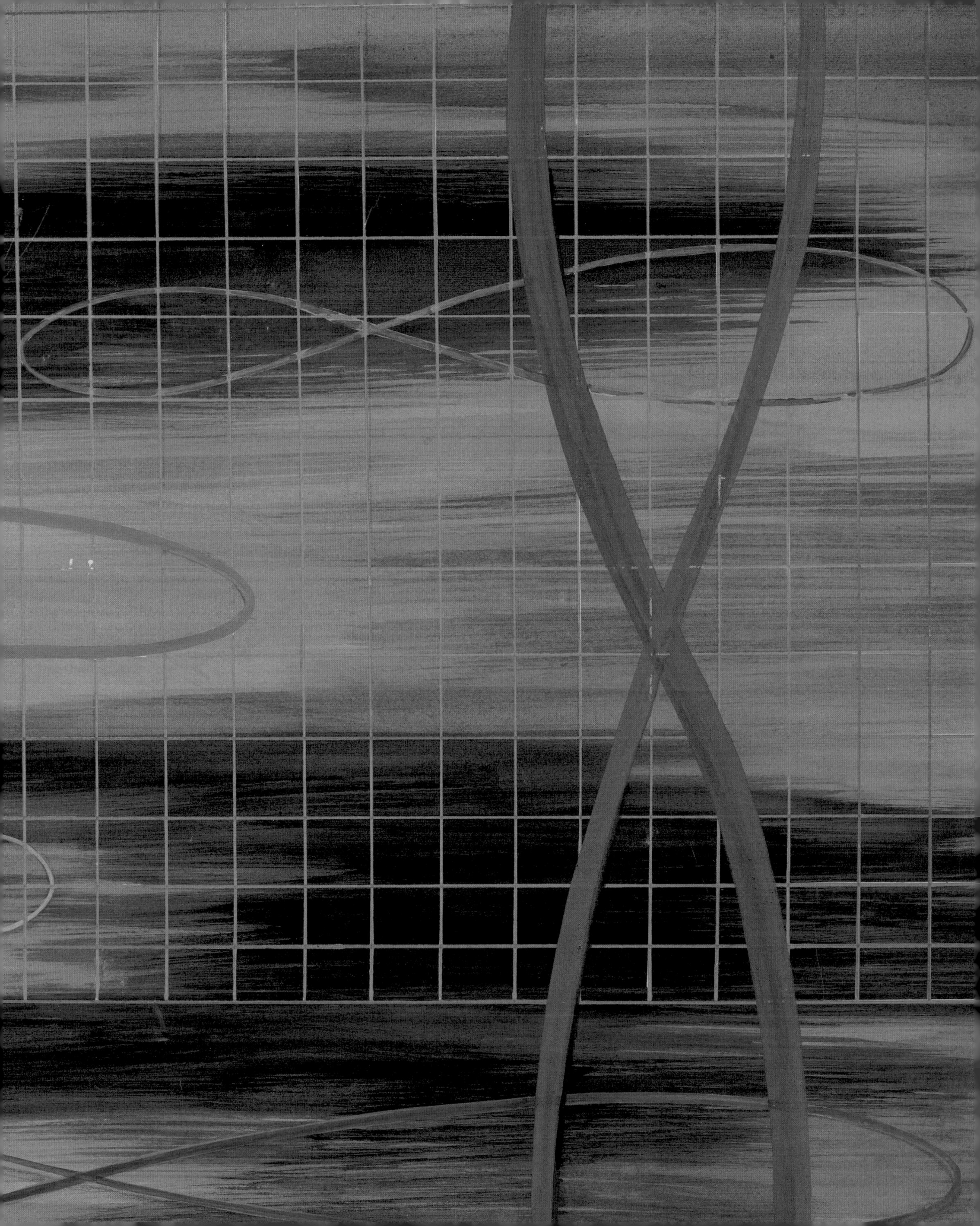

War Commentary: Questions and Conjectures

Current knowledge of Henry Eveleigh's practice offers no evidence of a work by him exhibited under the title *War Commentary*. This was the name borne by this work when it was acquired by the Montreal Museum of Fine Arts in 2015, but it was likely not original. It seems reasonable to assume that the artist exhibited the picture under another title and that it was almost certainly included in the major 1942 exhibition *Paintings by Louis Muhlstock and Henry Eveleigh,* in which the artist showed at least three works whose subjects were directly related to war. Based on descriptions given by critics of those works, whose present fate is unknown, I would like to propose a few hypotheses without, however, providing any firm answers.

In the summer of 1939 the Art Association of Montreal held an exhibition that brought together fifty contemporary Montreal artists. Robert Ayre reviewed the show in the 1 July issue of the *Standard*, and his brief descriptions include the following: "Henry Eveleigh's reportage – newspaper, planes, searchlight, bombs – Shanghai 1937."[1] Ayre's description is obviously too telegraphic to identify the work he saw conclusively as *War Commentary*, even though several elements – newspaper, airplane, bombs – are common to both. Also, the two red circles seen on the wings of the plane in *War Commentary* typically adorned Japanese war planes.

Eveleigh was born in Shanghai, and, according to certain sources, after studying in Europe he taught in that city at the Henry Lester Institute of Technology in 1937 and 1938,[2] just before immigrating to Canada. In 1937, Shanghai was the scene of a major battle of the Second Sino-Japanese War that pitted the Republic of China Air Force against the Imperial Japanese Navy. In August 1937 the air force of the Japanese Navy embarked on one of the conflict's first strategic bombing campaigns. Thousands of Chinese civilians were killed. Was this early air strike also the subject of the painting exhibited in 1942 under the title *First Air-Raid*?[3]

ill. 47
Henry Eveleigh
War Commentary, about 1938–39